ADVENTURES ON THE HIGH SEAS

ADVENTURES

MEN IN ACTION SERIES
Union Pacific   *Garry Hogg*

 WALKER AND COMPANY/New York

ON THE HIGH SEAS

TRUE SEA STORIES FROM CAPTAIN BLIGH TO THE NAUTILUS

DOUGLAS REEMAN

First published in the United States of America in 1971 by the Walker Publishing Company, Inc.

ISBN: 0-8027-6088-0

Library of Congress Catalog Card Number: 70-166181

Printed in the United States of America from type set in the United Kingdom.

To John Arthur Morgan

Contents

Illustrations

ACKNOWLEDGMENTS

The author acknowledges the following for use of photographs
in this book. Plate 1 is taken from *The Kon-Tiki Expedition* by
Thor Heyerdahl, published by George Allen & Unwin Ltd.
Plates 2, 12, 14 and 15 supplied by Syndication International.
Plates 3, 4, 5 and 6 supplied by Thomson Newspapers Ltd.
Plates 7 and 8 supplied by The Radio Times Hulton Picture
Library. Plates 9, 10 and 11 supplied by the Imperial War
Museum. Plates 16, 17 and 18 supplied by the Royal National
Lifeboat Institution.

Foreword

Since time began, and man first looked beyond his own coast or shoreline, the sea has represented both challenge and inspiration. It has been all things to all men, and its grandeur and majesty have been matched only by its latent power and cruelty.

To the passing holidaymaker or carefree dinghy sailor the sea can be a backcloth to other, more personal pleasures. While to the half-frozen, salt-blinded trawlermen in the bitter wastes of the Arctic it is the common enemy, one which waits with relentless patience to pluck away a foot or handhold, to overload the little ship with top-ice and capsize her into the depths.

It would, of course, be quite impossible to include in a book, or for that matter a whole regiment of them, all the exploits of the men who have challenged the seas and the oceans of the world, down through the records and memories of time. It would be an impertinence even to attempt it.

The stories of the men and their various craft who have faced the hazards of the ocean are legion. I have selected just a few, as varied as possible, in an effort to mark the progress and the failures of those who have accepted the challenge as best they could.

The reasons for the maritime episodes are as mixed as the men who made them into history. For trade or for colonial development and expansion. To wage war and to carry help and succour to the end of the earth when it was most needed. There are those who see the challenge as a personal thing, an obstacle to be overcome, like a race or a record of physical endurance. Some have faced the unknown out of necessity and from fear. All, except perhaps the foolhardy, have understood the sea's greatness, what it can offer, and just as easily take away.

Some of the episodes I have included concern war, for the sea is timeless and makes no allowance for man's petty differences and ambitions. Some are of those who give their lives to helping others in distress, no matter at what cost to themselves.

Yet so many have been left out, but are not forgotten. The deep-sea fishermen and the ordinary day-to-day sailors in a hundred different types of vessel who face danger each time they venture from harbour or dock. The men who crew the weather ships and those who keep a constant vigil from isolated light-vessels. The ships come and go like shadows, carrying the necessities of life we too often take for granted. Each has a story to tell, just as every day the sea throws up some new challenge and puts another barrier against man's determination.

To all those who have gone down to the sea before us, and those who even now are setting off for the first time, this small collection of episodes is humbly dedicated.

DOUGLAS REEMAN

I

Six Men on a Raft

On the 28th April 1947 the ungainly raft named *Kon-Tiki* was towed out of Callao harbour in Peru, and once clear of the port limits was freed to take her chances in the vast expanse of the Pacific Ocean. Of the many thousands who watched from the shore few ever expected to set eyes again on the raft, or her crew of six men and a raucous green parrot.

During the months of feverish exploration and planning the warnings and advice showered upon the would-be explorers had been as predictable as they were unnerving. It could not be done. It was foolhardy and impetuous. It was a criminal waste of human lives.

But the young Norwegian who commanded the strange craft, Thor Heyerdahl, although not a professional seaman, had taken plenty of time to prepare himself for the voyage. To him it was not merely an adventure or a test of endurance, it was the one and only sure way to prove a theory which had been in his thoughts for many years.

Perhaps it had all started some ten years earlier on the small island of Fatuhiva in the Marquesas Group, 4,300 miles from South America, when Heyerdahl had been busily collecting relics of a dead culture. There, as he sifted and searched for information and forgotten re-

mains, he became more and more convinced that there
was a strong connection between the peoples of the
islands of Polynesia and the extinct civilisations of Peru.
Tribal carvings and records took his research back in
time just so far, but then ceased entirely. He spoke to old
men, listened to their mixture of history and myth, all of
which strengthened his earlier belief that the Polynesian
islands had originally been peopled by refugees fleeing
from Peru.

It was said that Tiki, a great god and chief, had
allegedly brought his peoples to the islands across thousands of miles of ocean, and Heyerdahl had already discovered vast stone figures of Tiki which closely resembled
the giant monoliths which are accepted relics of a lost
civilisation on the South American mainland. But if this
was so, how did they reach there?

It was also known that when European explorers first
landed in the islands they were met by pale-skinned, tall
and handsome natives, who had well-found stone buildings and roads, and whose livestock contained pigs and
fowls as in any established colony.

At the outbreak of the Second World War when
Norway was occupied by the Germans, and while Heyerdahl left his peaceful pursuits to do his military service,
the problem and the growing theory were never far from
his thoughts.

As soon as the war was over, and in spite of the open
criticism and scorn for his ideas, Heyerdahl set to work to
put his theory into practice. Tiki had crossed from Peru
with his peoples on crude open rafts made of balsa logs, or
so it was said, and so then would he.

Not surprisingly, the harshest attacks on his plans were
made by those who lived from the sea, the professional

seamen, men who had learned the hard way not to take chances or to mock the power of their common enemy. Balsa logs were very porous. Therefore they would soon become waterlogged and sink. That was all there was to it.

Heyerdahl argued that if balsa had floated in A.D. 500 it was good enough for him also.

Others said that the great logs, once lashed together, would soon work and grind in any sort of a sea and the ropes which held them would chafe and part, throwing the occupants and their lives to the sharks.

Yet in spite of the storm of criticism bit by bit and a step at a time Heyerdahl began to win support. Perhaps it was his grit and determination as well as his obvious sincerity which began to hold and influence others, rather more than any lessening of a firm contention that his scheme was still doomed to early failure.

And so as months passed and the need for urgency increased because of the possible change in weather conditions, the raft began to take shape. By no stretch of the imagination could it be described as beautiful, but Heyerdahl and his five companions were determined that it should be an exact replica, and only a small radio set to keep contact with the outside world was allowed to break this rigid code of authenticity.

The raft was constructed of five big logs, pointed at the forward ends. The longest measured forty-five feet, and the shorter ones which made up the sides of the raft were thirty feet in length, the whole being lashed together with hemp. Authentic to the last degree, it did not have any nails nor an ounce of metal to assist with its durability or comfort.

The beam measured eighteen feet, and at the after end they constructed a cabin or hut eight by fourteen feet which was to be their shelter and home, and, if the gloomy onlookers were to be believed, their tomb also.

There was a square canvas sail on a short double mast, which coupled with a pine centreboard and a long, cumbersome steering oar would give them some sort of control once they were clear of the land.

Heyerdahl was convinced that if the raft could stay on the Humboldt current they had every chance of reaching their goal. The Humboldt current carries the cold masses of water from the Antarctic along the coast of Peru and then west again towards the islands. He was also certain that the ancient rafts of Tiki had followed the same route. Pulled by the ocean current, pushed and propelled by wind and sea, they had done what no sailors had achieved before or since in living memory.

The provisioning of the raft was a real problem, for no one had any firm idea of how long the voyage would take. Heyerdahl and his crew decided eventually on rations for six months. They also loaded 250 gallons of fresh water in fifty-six cans, as well as fruit and coconuts, all of which had to be stowed and lashed throughout the raft with great care in order not to influence its stability.

Fishing gear and shark repellent, sextants and charts, and finally a tiny rubber dinghy were somehow wedged, tied or dangled on or over the strange-looking vessel, and they were ready to go. Or as ready as anyone could be who was stepping out into possible oblivion.

It was almost as if the sea itself was trying to deter them at the very last moment, for during the first sixty hours it attacked the raft with unexpected fury and persistence. The motion was brutal, and as the *Kon-Tiki* rose awkwardly above the roaring wave-crests it took several hands on the steering oar to keep the stern end-on to the sea.

Already the balsa was rapidly absorbing water, but in one thing at least the early critics were confounded. The ropes, instead of chafing themselves apart in the sickening motion were biting deep into the soft balsa logs so that they were protected and not exposed as gloomily predicted.

All the same, there must have been someone aboard who pondered the sense and reason of the venture in those testing and savage moments.

As the hours dragged by, and Heyerdahl and his crew struggled amidst spray and wind, one other fact suddenly became clear. The *Kon-Tiki* had not been smashed down by any of the white-fanged waves, but had risen up and over each one before sliding dizzily into the next eager trough. The raft was not falling apart, and except for the unaccustomed effort and the perverse behaviour of the steering oar, they were holding their own. More than that . . . they were on their way.

With the coming of better weather and calmer seas they were able to contemplate at last the full meaning of their mission. From horizon to horizon the sea was theirs. No shipping lanes and nothing but the blue vault of the sky above and the great glittering expanse of water on every hand. Yet they were not alone entirely. Attracted perhaps by this strange newcomer in their midst, the fish cruised close by, their shapes and colours defying every description. Blue shark and sardines, tunnies and bonitos, with the madcap dolphins in almost permanent company.

Flying-fish, fleeing from one enemy or another, would leap and land helplessly on the raft, and were soon found to make excellent eating. In fact at each new dawn all the cook had to do was gather them up like an overnight harvest and lay them on the primus stove.

At night the sea changed again. The two helmsmen, straddle-legged and held in safety by their lifelines, would soon be aware of nameless black shapes which swum slowly to the surface, soundlessly watching before sinking again into the depths. Or the round, hypnotic stare of great luminous eyes, like those of the Old Man of the Sea himself. The latter were known to belong to the giant squid, curious only of the raft perhaps, but nevertheless to be treated with respect.

Never a day passed without witnessing some fierce battle. Shark versus dolphin, or shark against shark, ending in bloody turmoil within feet of the raft.

The sharks were always with them, sometimes playful, continually watchful, with their green cats' eyes skimming around or under the raft, their five or six rows of razor-sharp teeth gleaming in constant ambush.

The six young seafarers, bearded and tanned already like shipwrecked mariners, never had much time to be bored. They were even visited by one of the rarest and certainly the largest known fish left alive, the great whale shark. They average fifty feet in length, and their fifteen-ton bulk can churn the surface like a miniature submarine. But having carried out a cursory inspection of the raft the great fish dived and vanished once more, leaving them with the smaller but more dangerous followers for company.

Several times Heyerdahl and his companions harpooned the sharks which became too careless or too eager for the tasty bait of hooked dolphin meat, and in those moments everyone had to move in quickly in order to avoid the snapping jaws and lashing tail until the beast was finally overpowered. Normally on these occasions the raft's green parrot would cling to the rigging shrieking with obvious enjoyment or alarm according to the way the contest was progressing.

After forty-five days at sea the *Kon-Tiki* had covered two thousand miles without sighting a ship or even a speck of land. They had not merely survived, they had rather become a close-knit team. It says much for their good humour and compatibility that they were able to exist, let alone prosper, on their tiny island of balsa logs, for as in any small craft out of sight of land for long periods, little idiosyncrasies can become real irritations, petty differences can flare up into open conflict in a very short time.

The fact was that they were always busy. With two constantly on watch at the helm, the others were engaged in the many jobs of keeping their daily routine up to date. In the little cabin with its roof of banana leaves and bamboo-plaited walls someone would be working on the charts or tinkering with the radio set. Outside on deck the duty cook would be preparing the next meal, while another might be resting or preparing a lashing or splicing a frayed piece of rigging.

At night as they slept they were often awakened by larger fish scraping beneath the logs, their fins and tails barely a foot away, and must sometimes have wondered at the fates and ideals which had carried them this far.

As in any long sea voyage there were moments of carelessness which might, and nearly did, end in tragedy.

On one such occasion they had lowered the small rubber boat with no other purpose than 'to see what they looked like'. The first two paddled clear of the raft, and when they returned they had to be hauled aboard because they had become prostrate with laughter. For the first time they had seen their raft exactly as it would appear to a surfacing fish or an onlooker, had there been one. The logs had been hidden in the waves and only the hut was clearly visible from the tiny rubber boat. As Heyer-dahl later reported in his journal, 'it was like an old Norwegian hay-loft lying helpless, drifting about in the open sea'.

But the next attempt nearly proved fatal. As the boat paddled away in order that a photograph might be obtained, the wind and sea rose unexpectedly. The wind took a firm grip of the raft and hut and the drift increased alarmingly over that of the dinghy. For some moments longer it looked as if they would never be able to battle their way back to the raft, and were faced with the horror of being left further and further astern, to die perhaps within sight of their friends who were powerless to help them. For unlike any other craft, the *Kon-Tiki* could not be halted or turned, nor could she manœuvre but for the most basic of movements.

On all the following occasions a lifeline was firmly affixed to the rubber boat and an eye kept for any sign of a change in weather.

Some might say that sort of incident should have been foreseen. But these men were amateurs, learning their new trade day by day with no yardstick to guide them. Their code of discipline was strange by most maritime standards, but somehow fitting for their very existence, where self-discipline carried far more value than the taking or giving of orders. Whenever a new problem arose they would gather in the little hut or on the open foredeck and talk it out. By this method they usually found the best and most reliable solution. After all, Tiki had left no handbook, and nobody else had attempted what they were doing.

At the end of two months the water supply had become stale and had an unpleasant taste, and although each man received only a quart each day it was often the case that it was not completely consumed. Curiously enough, salt tablets were almost more important, for under those conditions perspiration drained the body of salt in a very short while, as many shipwrecked sailors have found to their cost.

Heyerdahl had been advised that the nearer they got to the islands the worse the weather would become, but nevertheless the change came with breathtaking suddenness, a foretaste perhaps of what still lay ahead.

On the night of July 2nd the watch on deck found that they could no longer squat in comfort studying the sky and its great backdrop of countless stars. After several days of a light north-easterly the wind had risen in strength and the sea was broken and angry. As four men lay asleep in the cramped cabin, Heyerdahl, who was on watch, saw a giant sea bearing down from astern. As he later admitted, had they not just passed through that area he would have imagined it to be heavy breakers across some uncharted reef. But it was no reef, and the broken-crested wave stretched away on either hand as far as he was able to see. Worse still, he could just make out two more serried lines of waves following rapidly after the first. Seizing the steering oar and hauling with all his strength to swing the raft round to take what was coming he yelled a warning to his sleeping companions, and as they stumbled to their feet the first wave reached them. The raft lifted wildly and rose up and up on to the very crest of the wave. Through a great welter of foam and bursting spray the *Kon-Tiki* reeled over the crest, the bows climbing rapidly while the raft slid down into a black-sided trough. As the other two seas came crashing down around them it was all they could do to hold on, and the last assault managed to hurl the raft broadside to the waves so that water spouted up between the logs and in through the wall of the hut. The small cabin was flooded, and on the foredeck the bamboo wickerwork was blown open like a shell crater.

Then almost before they could regain their breath they saw the waves passing them, leaving them behind as they surged on into the darkness. The damage was surprisingly light, but it left them feeling both shaken and apprehensive.

It was not clear what had caused the three freak waves. Perhaps they were the result of some disturbances or up-heavals on the sea's bottom, but once again it seemed as if the sea was testing them, even preparing them for what was to come just two days later.

It was then that the first real storm found them. As is customary in those latitudes the change was as sudden as it was violent. The trade wind died completely, and where moments before had been blue sky and feathery white clouds was an angry ferment of black-bellied clouds and violent gusts which appeared to come from several directions at the same time so that steering became almost impossible.

Then the storm really burst over them, with the sea becoming a raging panorama of leaping crests and deep, threatening troughs. Some waves hurled themselves above the raft, twenty-five feet from crest to trough, while the wind screamed through rigging and hissed between the bamboo walls of the hut. The crew had to grope like blind men from one handhold to the next as they tried to secure their meagre stores and prevent the raft from ripping itself apart. Bent double, naked and frozen by the spray, they stumbled about in a world gone mad. They lashed cargo and secured the tiny radio, and when suddenly a heavy rain squall added its weight to the onslaught it seemed as if the voyage was about to end in one terrible disaster.

But as the raft lifted, tottered momentarily on the crest of each rearing wave before plunging down again, one more fact became clear to them. The *Kon-Tiki* was taking everything which wind and sea could hurl at her, and while they gasped and slithered on the groaning logs they felt the same sort of wild excitement they had known when they had challenged and beaten the sharks for the first time. It was a contest, a fight, another form of sport, and as before they had found that they were equal to it.

For several days they were hounded by bad weather, but by July 21st the wind had died once more and they were able to take stock of their condition. They had suffered two real storms, and not surprisingly the raft, like its occupants, was beginning to show signs of strain. It was getting weaker in the joints, the logs were working badly and moved independently in spite of their lashings so that walking and sleeping were made very difficult. The logs had become treacherous with wet seaweed, but as far as buoyancy was concerned were still holding their own. Heyerdahl had chosen them carefully. Not dried out like some people had advised him, but fresh and impregnated with sap. But for the sap the logs would have become completely sodden within weeks and sunk under them.

The rough weather and need for constant vigilance had taken their toll of the crew's reserves, and the fact that the green parrot had been lost overboard further added to a sense of depression.

They all needed one thing and one thing only to lift them from this feeling, and on July 30th it happened. In the far distance they saw land for the first time since leaving Peru. It proved to be Puka-puka, a first outpost of the Tuamotu Group. They knew they would pass well clear of the island, but the sight of it was enough.

The next day they sighted land again, and for three more days and nights, carried by wind and current, they moved slowly towards their goal. It was to all intents a perfect landfall. The island of Angatau, lush and seductive in green palms and marked here and there by pale, inviting beaches. After ninety-seven days on the *Kon-Tiki* it must have seemed like a miracle.

But as always the sea had one more cruel trick left to play. While the raft edged closer and closer Heyerdahl and his companions realised that the island was surrounded by what appeared to be an unbroken necklace of jagged, rust-coloured reefs.

Slowly and painfully, zig-zagging as close as they dared, they moved around the beckoning, mocking island, still unable to accept this last twist of bad luck and disappointment. It was not possible. There had to be a gap in the reef somewhere. But there was not. After three days of searching and near disaster on the waiting reefs they had to admit defeat. Worse, they realised the current had taken them once more in its grip, was carrying them past and away towards the ominous Takume and Raroia Reefs. This new hazard was one of the worst known in the whole of that sea area. Stretching fifty miles, they were spread across the *Kon-Tiki*'s course, like broken teeth, hungry for another victim.

The moment for jubilation and congratulations was past. Heyerdahl and the others had succeeded in proving the first part of their theory, they had crossed from Peru to the islands with nothing but the elements and their raft to sustain them. But that was over, it had suddenly become a question of remaining alive.

They trimmed their sail and laid the oar hard over in one last hazardous attempt to skid past the miles of reefs. Beyond the barrier they had the other islands beckoning to them like sirens, and when darkness finally closed down upon them they had been one hundred days at sea.

The next morning showed them that there was no chance of avoiding a final embrace. The waiting was over. It would be very soon, and there was still a lot to do.

They could see the turmoil of leaping waves breaking across the reefs, the placid islands beyond. It was unfair, as it was frightening, but it had to be faced.

Quickly they constructed a crude anchor by filling empty water cans with old batteries and scrap, and prepared to lower it at the last moment to try and slew the raft round for the actual moment of driving aground. As they worked with frantic haste their ears must have been tuned to the roar and sigh of breakers, their bodies constantly aware of the raft's quicker, more erratic motion as the undertow took it like an unseen hand.

The last signal to be sent from the *Kon-Tiki*'s radio said, 'Fifty yards left. Here we go. Good-bye.'

Then they struck, lifted and struck again. Few can remember what exactly happened next. It was a nightmare of terrible sounds and crushing waves, of tossing surf trying to tear the *Kon-Tiki*'s crew from their precarious hand and toeholds, while all the while the sea smashed over the logs, exploring, destroying and finishing what the reefs had started.

Battered and bruised, groping and falling across the jagged coral, the six adventurers found their way ashore. How they had managed to survive was a mystery and a miracle, but more than merely surviving, they had conquered, and as they reeled up the nearest strip of beach and dug their toes into warm, bone-dry sand they were torn between wild exultation and a great sadness for the raft which lay behind them on the reef like a memorial to their endurance and triumph. Mastless, with the cabin smashed to pieces and the deck a mass of tangled rigging and broken cargo, the *Kon-Tiki* was a wreck.

And so ended the Kon-Tiki expedition. The migration theory which started the train of events leading up to that great voyage was never proved. But the *experts* have been wrong in the past and will be again. What was proved was that native craft constructed of balsa wood could and did survive, and the ancient and primitive peoples were able to take immense voyages as Heyerdahl and his friends had done. But even if their theory had had no historical value at all, the deed was worth every ounce of their efforts, every hour of their courage.

In 1969 Thor Heyerdahl, accompanied by a small crew, set off in a papyrus-built boat named *Ra* from Morocco en route for Mexico. It was to prove that the ancient Egyptians could have crossed the Atlantic in similar craft thousands of years before Columbus, with nothing but the currents and the easterly trade winds to assist them.

Unhappily the first attempt failed when his boat became waterlogged and was in danger of sinking after covering 2,000 miles of the journey.

Heyerdahl was undeterred, and with his usual quiet determination set to work to prepare for another attempt. In May 1970, accompanied by a seven-man crew and a small monkey, he set sail in *Ra 2*, an eight-ton papyrus craft, from the port of Safi in Morocco.

After the incredibly short voyage of fifty-seven days he stepped ashore in Bridgetown, Barbados, tired but triumphant, one more of his theories proved.

2

Escape

It is often said that the peoples of the British Isles feel a true affinity with the sea and have salt-water in their blood. If this be the case, it is hardly surprising, since no Briton can ever be born more than eighty miles from it.

In times of war it has been particularly in evidence, and if others have given up when they have discovered nothing but open water at their backs, the British have treated the sea rather as an ally than as final proof of their own defeat. In 1940, as the British Army fell back towards the coast under the enemy's relentless pressure, the thought uppermost in the mind of every soldier was 'Just let me get to the sea and somehow I'll get home'. The story of the Dunkirk evacuation has since been described as a miracle, but in wartime such things are too often taken for granted. At sea the hazards are increased to terrifying proportions, yet ordinary men are expected to face them and make the best of whatever resources are immediately available, not least being courage itself.

Many stories are recorded of fantastic feats of survival. In open, unprovisioned boats on the broad Atlantic or with nothing but a tiny raft or rubber dinghy to sustain life until safety could be reached.

In February 1942 the Japanese Army crossed the

narrow strip of water which separates Singapore Island
from the Malayan mainland, and the defending British
and Commonwealth forces were faced with total extinc-
tion or surrender. As far as the Japanese were concerned
it was a whirlwind, and in many ways unexpected,
victory. In three months they had invaded the northern
shores of Malaya, swept down the peninsula and destroyed
or captured all who stood in their path. A great deal has
already been written about the causes of this military
catastrophe, of the over-confidence and apathy, of out-
dated plans and an ill-founded belief that if the enemy
ever came he would come by sea and never overland.
These matters are not our concern here. This is the story
of a handful of men who rather than face the misery and
humiliation of capture decided to make their way to freedom by sea.

It was no Dunkirk. There was no friendly Kent across
a narrow English Channel, and no armada of courageous
small craft available to rescue the hard-pressed garrison
of Singapore.

All the large ships had long since left the island or had
been sunk in battle. Air-cover was non-existent, and the
time for complete surrender to the Japanese commander
was hours rather than days away. Many of the vessels
which had attempted to leave Singapore with troops and
evacuees had been bombed and sunk before they had lost
sight of land, communications had broken down, and it
was almost impossible to discover the exact whereabouts
of enemy warships or the full extent of the Japanese
domination.

But at Telokayer pier one small wooden motor launch
prepared to slip her moorings and take the one slim
chance left open of escape.

M.L. 310 was commanded by Lieutenant 'Johnny' Bull of the Royal Naval Volunteer Reserve, and in addition to one other officer and a crew of ten ratings he was to carry some very important passengers. A Rear-Admiral, an Air Vice-Marshal, plus their combined staffs of thirty officers and men. The voyage he was busily planning and charting was precarious enough for such a small and fragile craft, but with every inch of space crammed with extra passengers it had already taken the odds against him.

He had decided to make for Batavia in Java, the nearest location which as far as he could tell was not yet occupied by the enemy. Five hundred and fifty miles of dangerous, hostile seas in a vessel more used to patrolling within sighting distance of the shore.

On February 13th at 11.15 p.m. Bull gave the orders to cast off. It was a grave and anxious moment for both crew and passengers. For not only had they the prospect of the voyage and all its dangers to contemplate, but also they were very aware of the destruction and despair they were leaving behind.

The night sky was aglow from countless fires which burned in the town, and the waterfront buildings stood out stark and black against an inferno made by the air and artillery bombardments. It was like a scene out of hell.

Bull did not have much time to consider the grim spectacle for he was too busy conning the M.L. clear of the port. It was a hazardous business, for the smoke from the blazing buildings and a total absence of navigational lights made each yard of the way seem like a mile. The narrow channel was littered with wrecked ships, either partly submerged or lying just beneath the surface. There was drifting debris and floating logs, any of which might strike the M.L.'s hull and hole it.

They had to feel their way like blind men, with two sailors lying in the bows ready to shout aft to the bridge and warn of any approaching object.

On the tiny bridge Bull passed his helm orders and continued to manœuvre his command through the littered channel, his eyes probing the darkness, his ears shut to the menacing rumble of gunfire and the crash of falling buildings.

Then one of the steering wires to the rudder parted, and as the M.L. idled quietly with her engines stopped, some hasty and makeshift repairs were carried out. Soon they were moving again, but the smoke was thicker, and in the darkness it was likely they had drifted during the repairs to the steering. Anyway, shortly afterwards the M.L. lurched hard aground. Bull used all his skill in an effort to get her free. By putting the engines full astern and by moving the packed crowd of passengers from one part of the hull to another, but all to no avail. She had run aground on the Takong Reef just outside the port waters.

It was obvious that the M.L. would remain fast until the tide lifted her off in the morning. And by that time it would be nearly daylight, with the skies soon alive with hunting aircraft, searching for men such as Bull and his companions who were foolish enough to think they could escape.

If Bull thought about the possibilities of failure he did not show it. His responsibility was to get those people to safety and not to fight against hopeless odds, and any sign of despair on his part might have finished the voyage there and then.

At six o'clock in the morning the tide reluctantly allowed the hull to move clear, and Bull headed at twelve knots for the Durian Straits to the westward. He

knew that at any moment he might sight an enemy ship
or aircraft and to press on in broad daylight would be
madness. A few hours later he conned the M.L. inshore
of the island called Sugi Bawah and sent every available
man over the side to hack down palm fronds and drag
them back on board so that the hull could be camouflaged
and made to blend with the land. Beneath their canopy of
netting and fronds they watched the regular procession of
searching aircraft overhead. Maybe the enemy already
knew the M.L. was in the vicinity. There had been spies
and informers in plenty at Singapore, and perhaps the
Japanese had aerial photographs to show them if any
vessels had become missing overnight. The worst of it was
that because of the grounding they had made only thirty-
five miles out of the total 550.

In the evening they took down their camouflage and
weighed anchor. Under cover of darkness the M.L.
slipped through the Berhala Straits, keeping the engines
throttled down because it was known to be a well-
patrolled area, and when dawn found them again they
dropped anchor off Katjangang in the group known as
the Seven Islands. It was another nerve-racking day,
with droning aircraft above and several sightings of
smoke on the horizon to show of the enemy's efforts. In
their cramped quarters the men lay about sleeping or
chatting quietly, and some wrote letters, although with
little hope of their ever being read.

Bull consulted his chart and at dusk got the craft under
way once again. This was to be the most dangerous part
of the voyage in many ways. He had to take the M.L.
across thirty-five miles of open water and around Banka
Island, this was close to the south-eastern corner of
Sumatra, which had already proved to be a journey's end

for many of those who had tried to escape from Singapore,
and was heavily patrolled by the enemy.

They had been moving for less than an hour when the
lookouts reported four ships steaming purposefully from
the direction of Sumatra. Two of them were large cruisers,
the others destroyers.

Like most times when danger is expected it came as a
shock nevertheless. Bull ordered the helm hard over and
rang down for maximum speed, swinging the craft round
and heading back towards the same islands they had just
left. As the revolutions mounted and the M.L. gained her
utmost speed of twenty knots, every available pair of
glasses was trained on the distant warships. It was a
critical moment, but with the M.L.'s past luck it was still
possible they might avoid detection.

But it seemed as if the luck had run out. The rearmost
destroyer in the line of ships appeared to shorten as she
turned away from her consorts and started to head directly
towards the M.L. That was not all, for as Bull kept his
small craft pounding for the islands, five Japanese sea-
planes were sighted, close down above the sea like flying-
fish. Only one of them actually closed with the M.L., and
after it had received a fierce burst of automatic fire sheered
off unexpectedly to rejoin its companions.

The pursuing destroyer was coming up fast, the range
falling away rapidly until the watching seamen on the
M.L.'s deck saw the telltale flashes as she opened fire with
her forward weapons. The shells straddled Bull's craft,
throwing tall water-spouts high into the air, and had the
land been any further away the Japanese gunners would
have settled the one-sided contest without any difficulty
at all.

Heading as quickly as he dared amongst the islands

1 Thor Heyerdahl's balsa raft, *Kon-Tiki*, halfway on its voyage across the Pacific

2 Alec Rose and his mascot, Algy, in *Lively Lady* within two days of home

3 Francis Chichester in *Gipsy Moth IV* rounding the Horn under minimum canvas

Bull moved right inshore of the nearest one, while the destroyer went about and hurried back after the other three warships.

Bull guessed it was only a temporary respite, for the enemy knew they were there, and it was only a matter of time before more forces arrived to seek them out.

His first duty was to protect his passengers, so after running the M.L. on to a shallow strip of beach he sent them ashore without delay, so that even if the enemy returned the presence and whereabouts of the senior officers and their staffs would remain a secret.

With only two of the passengers remaining with the M.L. and her small crew Bull settled down to await events. He did not have to wait long.

It was another destroyer, and when she had closed the island as near as she dared she opened fire, dropping several shells on the beach and close to the grounded M.L. Then a boat was lowered, and under cover of the destroyer's guns moved smartly towards the shore. It was filled with armed seamen under the control of one junior officer.

While the Japanese landing party covered the M.L.'s crew with machine guns the officer questioned Bull and some of the others, but appeared satisfied that the M.L. was merely trying to escape from Singapore and carried no more people than her usual complement. There was another bad moment when the Japanese seamen started to search the hull, for Bull expected they would notice that there was far more bedding and stores aboard than were needed for his own crew.

It seemed as if the enemy destroyer was in a hurry and needed elsewhere. The young officer, very correct and polite, told Bull to leave the M.L. at once and join his men who were already lined up on the beach under the restless machine guns. Then, while the Japanese smashed vital machinery parts, radio and electrical gear, he informed Bull that the destroyer was too full of other prisoners and personnel and they would return later to collect the M.L.'s company.

As the boat returned to the destroyer, Bull was thankful for the young Japanese officer's presence during the search. It was quite common for the enemy to shoot those they could not take as immediate prisoners.

As soon as the warship had vanished, Bull and his crew set to work to try to repair the damage. For although it was serious, most of the men were so relieved to be still alive and free that they did not at first grasp its completeness. While the work of repairing and replacing fractured feed-pipes and ripped-out wiring went on, Bull went ashore to consult with the senior officers and other passengers. The latter had not been idle, and while they had been exploring the island had discovered a Dutch/Javanese observation post and its native commandant, who spoke good English and was able to give much local information.

Bull returned to his command to find that the worst had happened. The makeshift repairs would not hold out, and each time the main engines were started the fuel escaped so quickly that they stopped almost immediately. The hull had already received such a shaking from near misses that it too was beyond hope. Reluctantly Bell accepted that his command, M.L. 310, was done for.

The only other means of escape was the M.L.'s tiny dinghy, which was useless for the task. It seemed that there was nothing left but to wait meekly to be captured and taken back to join the many luckless thousands already behind barbed wire.

It was then that someone discovered the presence of an old native *prahu* lying battered and half-hidden on an adjoining beach. Fourteen feet in length, double-ended, with a maximum beam of four feet, she was in poor shape. The caulking had been done with tree bark, most of which had rotted away to leave great gaps throughout the hull. But to Bull and the others she represented one last tiny spark of hope. The wrecked M.L. would soon attract the enemy's attention again, so it was decided to move the *prahu* to another island close by to carry out repairs. It was all they could do to reach the other island without foundering, so how could they hope to cover the remaining 350 miles of their escape route? Desperate situations, however, call for desperate measures.

Bull was chosen to command the venture, and he had the unhappy task of selecting the small crew which would accompany him in the attempt to reach help. For out of the total of nearly fifty officers and men he would have room for only four apart from himself. He chose Lieutenant Pool, one of the passengers, and three ratings, Brough, Hill and Johncock.

They were soon hard at work. Tearing up shirts to caulk the open and withered seams and then smearing them with engine room grease was the first task. They stepped the small mast and repaired as best they could the crude, hand-made sail. The M.L.'s dingy brought stores across to the island, and these were stowed below the bottom boards to try to make the vessel as stable as possible.

Bull then made another difficult but sensible decision. If the *prahu* should be seen and stopped by a patrol boat they had to be able to deceive the enemy. He decided to take with him the Javanese commandant and his native assistant, who would pose as fishermen, while if required the others would hide beneath the bottom boards with the stores. The space available was only just over a foot deep.

Lieutenant Pool, who had already been injured, was asked to remain behind with the others. The three ratings tossed a coin for their own chances, and Motor Mechanic Johncock lost.

So on the afternoon of February 20th, one week after leaving Singapore, the small expedition was ready to leave. The crew consisted of Bull, Leading Seaman Brough, Able Seaman Hill and the two Javanese.

It was a moving moment for all of them, and hardly anyone spoke as they paddled clear of the island, and the crowd who were being left behind watched the frail *prahu*, knowing it to be their only hope of rescue. Jammed amongst the cargo of canned milk, coconuts, tinned meat, biscuits and a jar of fresh water was a bundle of hastily scribbled letters sent by those remaining on the island.

In addition to his precious navigational instruments Bull carried his revolver, a large White Ensign and a bottle of rum.

His hopes of getting well clear of the islands under cover of darkness were dashed as soon as the *prahu* was in open water. There was hardly a whisper of breeze to move the sail, so there was nothing else for it but to row. The craft had no rowlocks, so some rope loops were made to suffice while the three Britishers took turns at the long, awkward paddles or steered by the boat's compass which they had brought with them. The Javanese were unfortunately little help in matters of seamanship, being land natives and unused to the mysteries of boat-handling.

All night long they rowed and steered, while the two

natives slept in the bottom of the *prahu*, content, it seemed, to leave it to the experts.

Daybreak found them still without any sort of wind for their limp sail, and their hands and bodies ached from the constant efforts at the paddles. The sea was flat calm, and the sun blazed down mercilessly on their arms and bodies. They all wore wide-brimmed native hats, and but for them would have suffered even more. Once they sighted smoke on the horizon, but nothing came near. Bull guessed it was more likely the death pall of a torpedoed ship than any sort of patrol.

As the sun rose higher in the empty sky the heat became a torment, so that none of them could work at the rowing for more than fifteen minutes at a time.

And there was little time for rest either.

By late afternoon they had succeeded in reaching Banka Island, but even then there was no relaxation. The offshore currents were so powerful that they had to row all the harder to remain on the route Bull had picked out at the beginning of the voyage. If the wind had got up there would have been some respite and the sail would have eased the agony of rowing, if only for a short period. But the sea remained like blue glass, and the sun pinned down their frail craft on the flat surface without mercy.

For three days and nights they rowed and laboured at their oars, moving the *prahu* along the eastern side of Banka Island. Only in the cool of the night did they find some relief, although the actual work went on as strongly as before. Bull distributed the odd mixture of rations to his crew; condensed milk, coconuts and tinned meat, and kept an even more careful eye on the fresh water supply.

They had become quite used to their fragile craft, rowing and baling, eating and dozing in short relays, and all the while keeping a good lookout for any searching patrols. Several times they saw distant aircraft, but nothing happened. Bull had decided to keep as far out to sea as possible, and was content to keep only the heights of Banka Island in sight.

On the third day they neared the south-east tip of the island. Any pride and excitement which they might have entertained faded somewhat when they considered the next and final leg of their voyage. Two hundred miles from Banka to Batavia in Java, in a battered, leaking *prahu* which most people would have thought unsafe in the Thames Estuary.

Bull also had to consider the very real possibility that the voyage could run well over his planned time. They might fail to get any favourable breezes for the sail, they could also be pinned down by the enemy and consume more stores than he had expected. He made up his mind to take another risk and move inshore to replenish stocks. He was also short of one other essential commodity— information, and there was a chance he might be able to glean some from local natives, should they prove to be friendly and not too cowed by their new Japanese over- lords.

Passing the lighthouse at the island's tip they coasted inshore towards the little village of Laboe. Bull checked his revolver and watched anxiously while his men paddled the *prahu* for the beach, expecting to hear a challenge or the first rattle of gunfire from the peaceful-looking huts at the fringe of the nearby jungle.

But no soldiers appeared, and instead the *prahu*'s small company soon found themselves surrounded by native villagers who guided them ashore and made them welcome. As Bull and his companions were plied with food from the village cooking fires he decided to send the Javanese commandant in search of the lighthouse keeper, who might be able to supply more information about enemy forces than the hospitable natives.

By the time the commandant had returned Bull noticed that there was some change in the natives' attitude. They seemed on edge and timid, and coupled with what the commandant had discovered from the lighthouse keeper it seemed they were beginning to see the arrival of the *prahu* as a real embarrassment and no little danger to themselves. The Japanese were, it appeared, in control of Banka, and had already shown themselves to be totally ruthless with anyone who attempted to help escaping refugees from Singapore.

Bull and his men collected their extra cargo of coconuts and filled the water container, while the commandant and his Javanese assistant made good use of their local knowledge to wrap several parcels of smoked fish in leaves as a change of diet for the voyage ahead.

Bull paid the villagers for their food with some of the money he had brought with him on the voyage. This was not merely for the sake of kindness, but might deter a would-be informer from seeking out the nearest enemy outpost.

Setting the sail to catch an offshore breeze and paddling briskly they left the land behind them once more, rested and refreshed by the few hours' freedom amongst other human beings.

But when darkness had closed down, the sky became cloudy, and within minutes the wind rose alarmingly. Bull knew it was a tropical storm which had found them and ordered the sail to be struck. Paddling frantically to keep the *prahu* end on to the sea they were carried by wind and waves, conscious the whole time that the crests were getting higher and more threatening and the wind gusts growing fiercer every moment.

The little *prahu* was being hurled about like a piece of flotsam, the crudely patched seams working so badly that it took constant baling to keep her from foundering there and then.

Half-blinded with salt spray, bruised and battered by the pitching hull, they worked without let up, their hands raw and blistered from rowing, their senses dulled by the fierce squalls which swept down on them without warning again and again.

And that was how it was to continue. Sudden calms, with the damp rising from the *prahu* and their sunburned bodies like steam, followed by swift, savage storms and more agonising work to keep the *prahu* afloat and in one piece.

The bad weather made navigation even more difficult than before, and Bull knew that many of his calculations had become mere guesswork. The strong winds, the drift and the hours lost in baling and repairs made any true position uncertain, but at no time did Bull receive any hint of complaint from his companions. It says much for their trust in him and in each other that they were able to face the unfair contest of sea and wind and could still sing and crack jokes in spite of their discomfort.

Each man knew that the voyage was not merely one of survival or escape. Theirs was a mission. To reach friendly forces so that help could be sent to rescue those who still waited, helpless and trapped on the island where M.L. 310 had gone aground. Perhaps that knowledge more than any other was the strength which held them together.

At night it was hard to retain a true sense of direction

because the bad weather always seemed at its worst at that time. On the night of the 26th February their luck almost ran out when the *prahu* was hit by the biggest storm yet encountered on the voyage.

It started with a sharp, powerful squall which almost tore the mast out of the hull and thrust the *prahu* hard over into a trough even as the crew fought to tear down the sail and save themselves from being engulfed. With the great, broken waves rearing and plunging behind them and the wind whipping the spray from the crests like hail they fought with paddles and rudder to keep from capsizing and being driven under. They were being carried on at an alarming rate, baling frantically and clinging to the slippery hull to avoid going overboard. In addition to all this there was a real danger of being swept helplessly before the seas like a waterlogged branch until they became caught by the powerful current which sweeps between Java and Sumatra, known as the Sunda Strait. Once that happened Bull and his companions would be able to do nothing and would be carried at the mercy of the sea until they were wrecked or died from thirst or exposure.

They had already done more than was considered humanly possible, and had managed to avoid enemy patrols as well as overcome the constant hazards offered by the elements.

To reach this far and to fail was almost too hard to contemplate, and as they baled and rowed and faced sea after sea they must have thought the end was very near.

When the wind finally eased they laid on their oars with all their remaining will and strength, fighting against the dragging current in one final struggle to prevent the *prahu* being carried through the strait.

There was no sleep, although each man was almost

exhausted, and in spite of baling the bottom of the boat was so filled with water that for the men not employed at the paddles there was still work in plenty for their torn and blistered hands.

Even so, they were almost fearful of what the daylight might bring. A sight of land, some place which they might recognise, or instead the endless expanse of a jubilant, mocking sea.

As the dawn came up they saw a hazy hump of coast-line, though what or where it was remained open to conjecture. But it was land, and Bull knew that somehow they had reached the end of the voyage. With the daylight strengthening about their listing craft they paddled grimly towards the shore, watching for signs to tell them where they were after 350 miles in their small, open *prahu*.

A bay opened up through the morning haze, and there, etched against the dark green shoreline beyond, lay several anchored warships.

For a few moments longer they paddled closer, hardly daring to hope lest they should find themselves heading for ships belonging to the enemy and their hard and bitter journey to have been in vain.

But the flag flying above the nearest ship was British, the same as the one Bull had carried with him all those miles and which he now hoisted in the place of the small, much-patched sail.

A boat filled with armed sailors came hurrying towards them, and as willing hands helped the weary, sunburned voyagers into safety, Bull was already telling his story while the rescuers could only listen in amazed silence.

Once aboard one of the warships Bull discovered that he had not in fact reached Sumatra, but it was near enough. The anchored ships lay at Merak near the entrance to the Sunda Strait. It had been a close call, but he had done what he set out to do.

While he and his exhausted companions enjoyed their first proper meal and bath the preparations were started to mount the rescue operation for those still marooned. Bull asked that he be allowed to return with the first rescue attempt, but his request was rightly refused. He had given enough already.

Unfortunately the attempt to save the surviving officers and men from M.L. 310 never succeeded. The Japanese had obtained complete control of the area, and it was only after the war was over that their fate finally became known.

A good many died on the island, and the rest had indeed been taken prisoner by the enemy.

Bull's efforts to fetch help, the courage and determination of his companions made just a small story when the world was in the grip of great and terrible events.

It was, nevertheless, more than worth the memory, and the telling.

3

Single-handed

Sailing a yacht around the world, even when taking full advantage of the Panama and Suez Canals, is not a venture to be attempted without a good deal of thought and planning. With a trained crew, a well-found boat and both the time and finances to make such a voyage possible it still calls for considerable skill and tenacity.

To make an open-water circumnavigation of the globe *without* the benefit of the canals and completely alone must seem to most people an impossibility. The physical effort entailed to keep a small yacht on course, coupled with the mental strain of being alone for months on end in all weathers, must call for a very special type of person.

The single-handed yachtsman must know his boat like his own body, must have the feel of her so that he can drive her to but not beyond her own limit of endurance. He has to be prepared to replace broken gear, splice severed rigging and carry out any sort of repair from his own resources at any time of the day or night and with no consideration for his personal safety.

Navigation and the day to day routine of maintenance, as well as feeding and tending to his own wants leave little time for contemplation or second thoughts.

And there is always the lurking fear of illness or personal

injury. In heavy seas or even a sudden squall a lone sailor can break a limb or so injure himself that he can only watch helplessly as his boat is overwhelmed completely and driven under.

Yet as with all such challenges there are those who accept the odds and pit their skills and ability against whatever the sea has to offer in return.

The first man to succeed in circumnavigating the globe was Joshua Slocum in his little nine-ton sloop *Spray*. He set off alone from Boston in April 1895 having rebuilt his boat from a derelict hulk. The total cost of the materials and equipment required for making *Spray* fit for sea was a mere $553.62, plus thirteen months' ceaseless work with his own hands. Compared with today's sleek ocean racers costing many thousands of pounds, with their electronic devices and automatic steering, their lightweight sails and super strong rigging the *Spray* would seem primitive.

But Slocum knew his boat and his own skills, and was able to sail the *Spray* for many hours at a time with nothing more technical than a lashed helm and an inbuilt knowledge and awareness of the sea and wind around him. He crossed the Atlantic to Gibraltar and then recrossed it to sail slowly down the eastern coast of South America to fight his way through the Magellan Strait. Then at a more leisurely pace he traversed the Pacific to Australia and the islands in the Indian Ocean before returning to Boston in 1898. It was a tough and arduous voyage, much of the time he was well clear of shipping routes and was once a total of seventy-two days at sea without touching a port of any kind.

Again in 1938 virtually the same single-handed voyage was completed by Louis Bernicot in his forty-one-foot *Anahita*, but already others were watching and planning to attempt an even greater feat of seamanship. For far tougher and more dangerous than the track taken by either Slocum or Bernicot was that now known as the old clipper route. It rounds the notorious three capes—the Horn, dreaded over the centuries by all sailing men, Leeuwin and the Cape of Good Hope. Instead of the moderate and friendly trade winds of the tropical and semi-tropical zones, the route depends on the great westerly winds and gales of the Southern Ocean, aptly named the Roaring Forties. The old clippers, depending on fast passages to pay their way and carry their much needed cargoes to Liverpool and Bristol, to Cardiff and the Port of London, were made to face the savage fury of blustering gales and the mountainous seas around Cape Horn in order to maintain both speed and efficiency in a very competitive world. With the coming of steam and the advantages of the great canals they had to surrender to progress and are now no more than a memory.

The first man to complete this great voyage alone was the Argentinian yachtsman Vito Dumas in 1942. In his forty-two-foot ketch *Legh II* he completed his circumnavigation in thirteen months and eleven days. An astonishing feat of seamanship and navigation, yet one which passed almost unnoticed by a world torn apart in war.

Vito's knowledge of wind and tide were of paramount importance. Even today he is perhaps still unparalleled and some of his passages are worth noting.

Setting sail from Buenos Aires in June 1942 he headed for the Cape of Good Hope. After a short pause to replenish stores he made a record non-stop voyage of over seven thousand miles, by-passing Australia and on to Auckland in New Zealand. The time taken was 104 days in all kinds of wind and sea.

Next he sailed to Valparaiso and made a voyage of 3,000 miles in seventy-one days, rounding Cape Horn and back to his starting point of Buenos Aires.

As in all early voyages, food and fresh water were constant problems. Lack of storage space, the need to be able to prepare a nourishing meal in the shortest time under all conditions, meant planning the stowage and the selection to the last detail. To be too optimistic over speed and distance covered could mean starvation or dying of thirst. Overload the small confines of the hull and the lone sailor would lose the boat's stability, perhaps when it was most needed.

Timing too, then as now, was of great importance. To arrive off the Horn, for instance, too late or too early and the single-handed crew would be up against all the fury of that desolate and dreadful place and with no hope of aid if things went wrong.

A quarter of a century was to pass before others took up where Vito Dumas had left off. Looking back it seems a very long time in a world always ready to find adventure for those willing to take the risk. Perhaps the same war which had overshadowed Dumas' great voyage had left the world weary of excitement and peril heralding a new age of austerity and uncertain peace. Most people had had their fill of danger and wanted nothing more than to be left alone to sort out their lives in their own way.

But this state of affairs could not last for long. Man is a born adventurer. His livelihood, his very roots, have always depended on the yearnings for challenge and achievement.

In 1966 two such men prepared to set out separately to challenge and to beat Vito Dumas' record, to sail around the world on the same route as the great wool clipper ships which had long since vanished from the seas.

The first lone yachtsman to leave was Alec Rose, a Portsmouth greengrocer, in his elderly cutter *Lively Lady*. Rose was later to capture not only the admiration and pride of those who followed his voyage but was also to give people something more. Something they could all understand even if they could not describe it. For quite unlike many of the long-distance yachtsmen in their heavily sponsored boats, their dazzling array of modern and sophisticated equipment, Alec Rose was the quiet, self-contained man so beloved in any seafaring nation.

Rose knew his boat and had dreamed of making his voyage around the world for many years. Like *Lively Lady* Rose was no starry-eyed youngster, and by the time he was ready and able to make his lone attempt was close on sixty years old. Not only did he know his boat, he also understood the sea, and had learned its cruel habits the hard way. During the Second World War he had served in the Royal Navy, for much of the time in the North Atlantic where the U-boats and hard-pressed convoys fought their endless and unremitting struggle to a bitter conclusion.

Physically Rose was not a strong man, and as a schoolboy had been deprived of the pleasures of sports and games because of his health. But what he lacked in perfect health he made up for with tenacity and a firm determination which was later to carry him and his *Lively Lady* right around the world.

The war treated Rose harshly. He was trained as a ship's engineer, and any sailor will tell you that in wartime it is the most testing and relentless of all jobs afloat. Down below in a rattling, roaring world of machinery there is little to warn you of the perils above and around

4 Robin Knox-Johnston in *Suhaili*

5 Donald Crowhurst's *Teignmouth Electron* alongside the *Picardy*, the ship which took her in tow

6 Interior of Donald Crowhurst's abandoned *Teignmouth Electron*

that enclosed existence. Only the sudden clamour of telegraphs, the demanding dials swinging from reduced speed to *Full Ahead* can tell the engineers of approaching danger.

Then there were the depth-charges which the small escort vessels dropped in thousands in their efforts to keep the prowling submarines away from their helpless charges, the merchant ships. Up on the wind-swept decks or open bridge it was bad enough, down below it was a living nightmare. Each time a depth-charge exploded it felt as if the ship had received a kick from an ocean giant, and in every engineer's mind was the real fear that the next explosion would be an enemy torpedo. Sealed in their noisy, steel world below the ship's waterline they all knew there was little chance of escape if that happened. The great inrush of water, the scalding horror of escaping steam, and then, with luck, instant oblivion.

Many men were worn out by such strain and personal danger, and Rose was one of them. When the war was almost finished he was invalided out of the Navy as a lieutenant in the Royal Naval Volunteer Reserve, his nerves in shreds, his mind dogged by the memories of what he had seen and endured.

But if his health had suffered, his will and determination remained as strong as ever. Over the post-war years as he built up his own prosperous little business he thought of his great idea and dream, and saved every available penny to make that dream become a reality. He went without many things which we might regard as necessary luxuries. But to Rose the freedom to sail, to be his own master was the only luxury he wanted.

In his spare time he went sailing in a small boat or watched the constant movements of shipping in the Solent.

He saved and he planned, and eventually purchased the cutter *Lively Lady*. She had been built nearly twenty years previously in Calcutta and was seaworthy rather than beautiful. Thirty-one feet long on the waterline, she was solidly built and constructed by men who had put stability and strength before a passing beauty.

The first real test for both man and boat came in 1964 when Rose took part in and completed the single-handed Transatlantic Race, a trial of strength and skill as well as a challenge from the ocean which had tried so hard to break him in the past.

He made further alterations to his sail plan, and heard advice from some of the best brains in the yachting and deep-water sailing business. It took a lot of time and most of his carefully hoarded savings, but nothing made him deviate from his goal, even though it was well known that another man, Francis Chichester, was also preparing to make the very same voyage in a brand-new yacht, *Gipsy Moth IV*. The nation's press seized the remarkable coincidence of a double attempt to circle the world and called it a race. In Rose's home port, Portsmouth, several influential people suggested forcefully that Rose should be sponsored by their city to provide him also with a new craft, one fitted with all the latest gear and designed for the very purpose of that staggering voyage.

Rose declined all their offers. He knew his *Lively Lady*. He had the *feel* of her, and that was that.

To get so far in his preparations, to see his years of planning and dreaming almost come to nothing at the very last moment, might have broken a lesser man. For Rose's venture seemed plagued with bad luck, and there were many who gloomily suggested it was only a foretaste of things to come.

There were failures and minor accidents, and then when he eventually set sail to begin his voyage he was run down by a steamship in the Channel and narrowly avoided having his boat destroyed beneath him. The collision happened at night, and although Rose saw the steamer's navigation lights bearing down on him he was unable to take much avoiding action as there was hardly any wind to fill his sails. He flashed a powerful torch again and again towards the other vessel's bridge but it was to no avail. The ship struck *Lively Lady* a glancing blow and brushed her aside like a piece of driftwood before steaming on into the darkness apparently quite unaware of what she had done.

Sadly Rose headed back to port, his beloved boat too damaged to start on a round the world voyage and his heart heavy with disappointment.

There was another disaster to follow. One day, at low water, and while *Lively Lady* was standing upright against a jetty wall, a mooring line slipped, and to the horror of several onlookers she toppled and fell crashing on to her starboard side cracking some timbers and doing other superficial damage.

Hiding his bitter disappointment from his friends, Rose made himself face one very certain reality. He would not be able to sail on time. The damage was too severe to be put right before the weather made the most dangerous part of the voyage impossible. There was nothing else for it but to postpone his attempt until the following year. With many hundreds of onlookers Rose watched Francis Chichester leave Portsmouth on 27th August 1966, listening to the cheers and the saluting sirens which but for his own cruel luck would have been for him.

While Rose got on with the job of repairing his boat and

prepared to sit out the long winter, Chichester in *Gipsy Moth IV* was doing his utmost to beat the past records with every ounce of skill at his command. The old clipper ships had made very fast passages. They had carried vast areas of canvas and had the necessary crews, usually up to some thirty officers and men, for all the work entailed. Chichester was alone and the task he was attempting had few yardsticks to guide him.

Gipsy Moth IV had been specially constructed at great expense for the task, yet even so Chichester's achievements were to stagger even the most experienced sailor.

His voyage around the Southern Hemisphere was nearly twice as fast as any which had ever been carried out by a small craft, no matter how large her crew had been. It was fantastic, and the film brought back by searching aircraft as Chichester rounded Cape Horn will be long remembered. That small yacht with a mere feather of sail in a vast, rearing wilderness of white-capped waves seemed to personify everything about man's constant battle with the sea.

Chichester's greatest distance between entering any sort of harbour was 15,500 miles from Sydney, Australia, back to Plymouth in Devon, double the record once held by Vito Dumas in *Legh II*. Even allowing for the more modern and better-equipped boat at his disposal, it was an overwhelming victory for Francis Chichester, who was later knighted by the Queen for his achievement.

Alec Rose could hardly be expected to beat this amazing record, and it is sad to relate that but for his run of bad luck he would have been able to make the first attempt, if not the fastest. *Lively Lady* was a twenty-year-old veteran and it would have taken another powerful vessel of the type designed for Chichester to make the odds at all acceptable.

Rose finally set sail from Portsmouth on July 16th, 1967, with the good wishes ringing in his ears but with no doubt in his heart as to what lay stretching before him.

But even the most optimistic person left behind on the shore would never have believed what was actually to happen. For in spite of everything Rose was to sail his *Lively Lady* around the world on the same route as used by the old wool clippers faster than any other yachtsman except Chichester. It was an amazing feat of seamanship and personal courage, both for an old boat and for her master who was approaching an age when most men think about retirement.

Rose's longest reach of non-stop sailing was shorter than Chichester's for he was forced to put into the New Zealand port of Bluff for repairs after *Lively Lady* had sustained some damage during the voyage, damage which was neither practical nor safe to be carried out at sea.

However, his lone voyage from England to Australia was twice as long as Vito Dumas' previous record of 7,200 miles. And one must remember that *Lively Lady* was no pleasure-cruising boat and certainly no ocean racer, so that this great feat of endurance had meant that Rose was required to face the harsh rigours of daily handling and commanding for many more hours than any man had done before him single-handed.

And as he sailed on and on around the world the hopes and prayers of the world went with him. Whenever his small yacht was sighted by passing ships or patrolling aircraft and the news of his position and progress were flashed across the radio and television networks in so many countries it was like a tonic to all those people who out of habit or circumstances were forced to stay at home in less-rewarding situations.

This great feeling of attachment which people had and still hold for this tenacious and stubborn sailor was built on many things. His efforts to overcome the early setbacks and ill-health, his very determination to win through in spite of everything, had made him into a sort of symbol. And perhaps almost as important his insistence from the start that he would do it alone, and without the obvious and readily offered help from rich and powerful sponsors like his predecessors and those who were to try to follow in his wake.

As he sailed closer and closer to the much-feared and respected Cape Horn his thoughts were busy with what he must face. It was the climax for any such voyage, and he knew that many great ships had foundered in attempting to beat around the Horn, ships fully crewed and expertly handled in days when such hazards were expected of sailors, if not actually taken for granted.

The lone sailor has all this to contend with and much more beside. After struggling with faults and storm damage, fighting against the constant lack of sleep and exhaustion, he is already near to the end of his physical and mental reserves. Yet the Horn is still there, the greatest challenge of all, waiting to throw its might and reputation against a man who has already given so much.

Rain, snow and fog made the going hard and navigation difficult, and the rough seas of the Southern Ocean made sure that *Lively Lady* would have no easy passage.

But even the sea seemed to have some respect for this remarkable man, for when the time came to make the final attempt the wind had fallen to a light north-westerly and the waves eased their pattern to drive the boat steadily on her way.

It is not hard to imagine Rose's feelings in those

moments. That great hump of land looming through the curtain of mist and spray, and he alone with his *Lively Lady* to see it. Cape Horn, the sight looked upon by so many seamen who had gone before. For many it had been the last sight they had seen on earth.

After resetting his sails and fixing a new course Rose went below to prepare himself a drink. One not only to sustain him, but with which to toast the occasion, the culmination of a great dream. Lemon, honey and a stiff tot of whisky was his choice, and somehow in keeping with this man's unbreakable, independent spirit. As he wrote in his log he must have smiled to himself. It was April Fool's Day, and he had not only fooled the Horn but everyone who had ever doubted his ability to get that far.

Three hundred and fifty-four days after leaving Portsmouth *Lively Lady* returned to a welcome which would make the strongest heart tremble. Sirens screamed, warships were dressed overall and the glittering Solent was covered with more small yachts and pleasure boats than had ever mustered in one place since Dunkirk.

To Rose, dog-tired, half-dead on his feet, it was like a dream. He still could not understand that he had won so much admiration and affection. He had not asked for it and, unlike some, had not expected it.

When he got his breath back he said, 'This makes one feel very humble.'

Then he was back on dry land, on Southsea Common, one of history's favourite patches. Where Richard II gathered an army for Spain and Nelson embarked for Trafalgar, and Queen Victoria presented some of her first V.C.s.

Rose was home, indeed he was within 300 yards of his little greengrocer's shop where his wife had continued to keep the flourishing business going as well as keeping friends and neighbours in touch with her husband's exploits whenever news was available from the other side of the world.

In his crumpled slacks and reefer, the jaunty but battered cap which had become so familiar in newsprint, he did not look much like a hero. It was hard even to get him to say more than a few words, and when he was told that he was to be knighted by the Queen for what he had done he was almost tongue-tied.

He did say: 'One must have the shadows of life to appreciate the light.'

Well, for Sir Alec Rose the achievement and the homecoming were all light and more beside.

Watching his return on television was a Mr Frederick Shephard, who had designed Rose's *Lively Lady* some thirty years earlier. Ninety-nine years of age, Mr Shephard also found great comfort and satisfaction in the events on that day in Portsmouth.

He said quietly, 'I feel very proud. I never had any doubts she would make it.'

Vito Dumas made a circle of some 20,000 miles around the bottom of the globe, mostly in the dangerous Roaring Forties. But the complete circumnavigation by sea which passes through two points diametrically opposite represents a voyage nearly half as far again.

Sir Francis Chichester in *Gipsy Moth IV* did it in nine months. Sir Alec Rose in *Lively Lady* followed close on his heels and completed the voyage in only eleven months. Different men and different boats, but their magnificent voyages were linked with the supreme strength of personal courage and an unbending will to 'go it alone'.

When such great and difficult voyages are undertaken

and completed with outstanding success it becomes harder
and harder to see where another challenger can head to
better past records. Yet in 1964, even as Alec Rose was
taking part in the single-handed Transatlantic Race and
preparing himself for his later and greater success, another
would-be challenger was already at work planning and
preparing.

Robin Knox-Johnston, a young Merchant Navy officer
who had just obtained his mate's ticket and had been
posted to the Indian coast for his shipping line, began to
build his own ketch, *Suhaili*. Always keen on the sea,
Knox-Johnston was nevertheless an individualist, and this
strong characteristic tended to make him somewhat of a
misfit in his early days as a young cadet when uniformity
was often considered both practical and more acceptable.

While still working on his thirty-two-foot-long ketch he
sat for and passed his master's ticket and was due to be
posted as Chief Officer on the London to Africa run. It was
a coveted promotion but placed him in an immediate and
unsettling quandary. He had spent all his available money
on the construction of his boat, and simply could not
afford the high price of having her shipped to England
with him.

Characteristically he decided to sail *Suhaili* home under
her own power, and accompanied by his brother and a
young Marconi radio officer as crew he set off for England
via South Africa, doing Durban to London non-stop.

His admiring young brother said of him: 'We were in
no doubt who was in charge. He never wore a lifejacket
and advised us not to wear one. *"If anyone goes over we'll
have no chance of finding him and a lifejacket only prolongs the
agony!"* '

With hindsight this might seem cold-blooded, but

sailors do tend to take this view when it comes to the balance between life and death at sea. It certainly shows that Knox-Johnston was already showing some of the inner steel which was to win him his well-deserved laurels later as a single-handed yachtsman.

After only a year as Chief Officer in the liner *Kenya*, Knox-Johnston came to hear that the French yachtsman Eric Taberley was planning a round the world non-stop attempt. It seemed to spark off something in his mind, perhaps this was what he had been wanting over the years, why he had built and fashioned *Suhaili* with such care and meticulous attention to construction and rig.

The past records had been achieved by others and he knew he could never be first with what had gone before. But to sail alone right round the world *non-stop*, without touching land for anything but the necessity to admit defeat, immediately appealed to him. And if anyone could or would do it first he wanted that man to be British.

This somewhat unfashionable outlook on a patriotic motive was variously received by both friends and family, but Knox-Johnston was quite sure that it should be done, and that he would do it.

His own company, the British India Line, were fortunately both tolerant and helpful. They gave him indefinite leave for the attempt, and on June 14th, 1968, he sailed from Falmouth in Cornwall on a voyage which was to make him the first lone sailor to circumnavigate the world, a total distance of 29,500 miles. The starting date was almost at the same time that he was awarded his commission in the R.N.V.R., so with one ambition already gained and in his pocket he was more than ready to tackle the next, the greatest challenge for any man afloat.

Quite unlike anything attempted by earlier round-the-

world yachtsmen, however, Knox-Johnston was being
confronted by more than the necessity to break previous
records. To attain his goal he not only had to circumnavigate the globe single-handed and without calling at a
single port, but also he had to do it against skilled and
determined opposition. The Sunday Times Golden Globe
award for winning the race had drawn a handful of the
best-known yachtsmen available, and each of those had
his own firm ideas about who was going to take the tempt-
ing record and prize at the finishing line.

His most dangerous adversaries were Lieutenant-
Commander Nigel Tetley in his powerful trimaran, and
the Frenchman Bernard Moitessier who had already distinguished himself as a first-class seaman and navigator.
There was also Donald Crowhurst in another trimaran
who was to vanish at sea in tragic and pitiful circumstances during the race.

With formidable dash Knox-Johnston drove his ketch
Suhaili without let-up from the first moment of sailing.
Within four months he was off New Zealand and the
watching world held its breath. He had already achieved
a notable and amazing voyage and had gone further than
any other lone sailor before him without putting into
harbour.

Calms and raging storms, adverse winds and perverse
currents, and yet he had driven on towards his goal. The
going had been far from easy. By November he had pulled
into calmer waters to take stock of his situation, and this
he was allowed under the rules of the race, but when
many people thought he might make an honourable
retirement from the contest he set to work to get his boat
fit and ready for the next leg. His self-steering gear had
been smashed, his fresh-water tanks punctured, and, even

more ominous, the *Suhaili*'s cabin was beginning to separate itself from the deck.

As he worked desperately to make temporary repairs, he tried to glean news of his adversaries, or those who still remained in the race. But accurate positions were hard to obtain exactly, and he still had to rely mainly in his own estimation as to where the closest challenger lay.

One thing is certain. It never occurred to Knox-Johnston to give up, and with the shortest possible delay he made sail once more.

This is the sort of attitude which separates the yachtsmen who work as a team from the real single-handed ones, the loners. Knox-Johnston was, and remains, an adventurer, one driven by the fierce and demanding sense of competitiveness like that which took Rose and Chichester on their remarkable voyages before him.

And by April 20th, 1969, he knew that but for some unforeseen and terrible disaster he had made it. After 310 days at sea in all conceivable conditions he was sighted less than ninety miles west of the Scillies. Without touching land and at an average daily quota of 95·2 miles he was almost home and dry.

And what of the remaining competitors? Lieutenant-Commander Tetley's trimaran *Victress* broke up and foundered only 1,200 miles from Plymouth after sailing 27,300 miles in 247 days. His daily average had been an impressive 110·6 miles. It was a heartbreaking disappointment, and the fact that his triple-hulled boat had broken up sparked off a whole series of arguments for and against that type of construction. He was awarded a consolation prize of £1,000 for his efforts and the fine achievement of his nearly completed voyage.

And while thirty-year-old Knox-Johnston prepared to

enter his home port he must have been reminded that if his other strong rival, Bernard Moitessier, had not decided to give up the race altogether, his boat and not *Suhaili* might well have entered a British port ahead of him. Exactly why the Frenchman decided to call off the race is not entirely clear. Maybe he felt that single-handed sailing meant just that. Alone, and with not even a competitor to break the demanding purity which he apparently required.

And the last competitor, Donald Crowhurst, what of him?

On July 10th, 1969, his trimaran *Teignmouth Electron* was sighted near the Azores. It was drifting helplessly and there was no sight of any living soul aboard.

It was thought that Donald Crowhurst had been swept overboard, and perhaps that was indeed the case. But when the trimaran's log was later examined there were even more distressing discoveries. All the while that Crowhurst had been radioing back his reports of his progress in the race, and the world's press had recorded it without question, he had in fact remained in the Atlantic. During the 243 days he was known to be aboard he was tacking back and forth in the Atlantic Ocean's emptiness with only his strange deception and inner torment for company.

Why he did it or what actually ended his life may never be known. It was a tragic end to a brave man, and one which brought home to many that other, unspoken danger which is always there to snare the lone sailor in the vast expanse of the ocean.

Typically, Robin Knox-Johnston summed it up when he said, 'Long-distance sailors will realise the strain Donald Crowhurst must have undergone. None of us should judge him harshly.'

Also typical of the sort of man who will always be on hand to challenge the sea, Knox-Johnston donated the whole of his £5,000 prize money to help support the dependants of the missing Crowhurst.

Suhaili was the only boat to finish the race, and Knox-Johnston's name is now where it belongs alongside those of Slocum and Dumas, of Chichester and Rose.

And the next voyage for the single-handed yachtsman, where will it lead, and who will attempt it? With men like these I am sure we will not have long to wait.

4

Bligh of the Bounty

On the morning of April 28th, 1789, a mutiny broke out aboard the armed transport H.M.S. *Bounty*, and her commander, Lieutenant William Bligh, with eighteen loyal companions, was seized, overpowered and then cast adrift in an open boat. At the time the ship was sailing between the Tonga and Fiji Islands in the South Pacific, and to those who remained aboard in comparative safety it must have appeared that Bligh and all those with him were being sent to certain death.

But as we shall see Bligh was no ordinary man, and was in no mood to accept what to most people would be a fate too terrible to contemplate.

Much has been written about the mutiny, but because many of the versions have been wildly exaggerated, some even totally false, it is necessary to touch briefly on the events which led up to the moment that small open boat was cut free of her parent ship. It is fair to say that had Bligh been alive in the present day he would have made far more money from slander and libel rightly awarded from film companies and writers than he ever made in a lifetime at sea.

His qualities, which failed to stop the mutiny, were those which not only saved the lives of his fellow castaways but also succeeded in completing a voyage which for length, privation and heroism is still unparalleled. For once cast adrift, Bligh was to take his small, overcrowded boat 3,618 miles to Timor in the Dutch East Indies with the loss of only one man, and that due to no fault of his own.

When the *Bounty* left Spithead in the winter of 1787 Bligh's orders were to reach the Society Islands and there take on board a large quantity of young breadfruit plants. These he would then carry to the West Indies for transplanting, in addition to any other useful plants and shrubs he might discover on his journey. Breadfruit had already been found to be as palatable and nourishing as bread itself, and it was expected, correctly as it later turned out, to grow well in the West Indies. There was a deeper and less-romantic notion behind the voyage. There were many slaves employed in the West Indies, their prime task being to ensure a regular and rich supply of sugar to England, and the breadfruit was to be their main source of food in the years to come.

The *Bounty* was hardly the most comfortable or spacious vessel for a voyage to the other end of the world and back again. She was only ninety feet long and twenty-four feet in beam, with a displacement of merely 215 tons. In addition to the many stores needed for her survival, she was further cramped by the stern cabin being rigged out as a floating garden for the expected breadfruit trees, with all the tubs, watering pipes and flower pots required to sustain them on their long journey.

Due to several unavoidable delays whilst fitting out for the voyage the weather was also turning against Bligh, and even to men used to the hardships of life at sea the *Bounty*'s quarters must have seemed very crowded. When she finally weighed anchor she carried a total company of forty-six, including David Nelson, a botanist, and his young assistant gardener to help care for the plants.

Because of the way which Bligh's character has so often been portrayed it is first necessary to obtain a picture of the man as he really was. At the time of taking command he was thirty-three years old, a prime seaman and officer, and one of the most experienced navigators in the Navy. He had been the Master of Cook's *Resolution* in his voyage of discovery to the South Seas a few years earlier. A Cornishman, Bligh had been first packed off to sea at the tender age of seven years and nine months, and was a professional to his fingertips.

We have often seen him shown as a bully and a tyrant, a man who delighted in punishing his men to a point of pure sadism. Yet in fact the records for flogging aboard his ship were minimal, and far less than might have been expected. It is strange to think that Captain Cook, who was as confirmed a flogger the Navy has ever had, got nothing but praise, whereas Bligh was condemned.

It is rarely mentioned that Bligh went to great lengths to care for his men's health, and throughout the first part of the voyage did all he could to ease the suffering brought on by foul weather and heavy seas. He had fires lit to dry out the ship and the seamen's clothes, studied their diet, and changed the normally accepted watch system aboard so that each man should get his maximum rest when below decks.

This is not to say that Bligh was a blameless saint. He had a zeal for efficiency which bordered on harshness, and was quick to show impatience for those who did not share his enthusiasm. He was given to sudden and passion-ate outbursts of temper and was unbending in matters of duty. When in a rage his language was offensive, but at the time was quite probably fitting. Naval service in those days was tough and demanding, and the seamen were often rough and coarse, even brutalised by their day to day existence in appalling conditions.

One of Bligh's failings appears to have been his lack of a real sense of humour, but when we consider his own hard upbringing at sea I think we might forgive him for that.

And if he was an impatient man he certainly seems to have had plenty to try that patience right from the beginning. The sailing-master, John Fryer, who was Bligh's second-in-command, was a dour, argumentative and totally unsuitable person for the exposed world of the *Bounty*'s quarterdeck. The surgeon, Thomas Huggan, upon whom Bligh had earlier relied to care for sick or injured seamen, was a drunkard and rarely able to leave his bunk. During the voyage a seaman died because of the surgeon's negligence, and this did little to ease the rift between officers and men, even though Huggan was also to die later himself, too drunk to realise what was happening right to the end.

And, of course, there was Fletcher Christian, a young, hot-blooded Manxman in his early twenties who was to play a vital role in the mutiny. It is ironic to realise that Christian was chosen by Bligh himself for the voyage, and had already served under him aboard another ship. As a master's mate, neither a commissioned officer nor a common seaman, he was in a better position than most to see the way things were going, and had he so wished could certainly have prevented the mutiny from starting at all. He did not so choose, and in fact became the mutineers' ringleader.

There can be little doubt that there was neither thought

nor talk of mutiny until the *Bounty* reached Tahiti in the Society Islands, almost a year after leaving England. Tahiti, with all it offered and represented, was the true cause of the upheaval which was to be discussed for many years to come.

It had been a hard and wretched voyage to reach that far. The weather had been so bad from the outset that Bligh had been made to give up his attempt to round Cape Horn and had had to recross the Atlantic to use the safer but more painstaking route around the Cape of Good Hope. For nearly five months the *Bounty* lay at Tahiti, and while the leisurely business of collecting breadfruit plants and repairing storm damage went on the ship's company discovered all the pleasures and the corruptions that a life of ease and plenty could give. After the harsh discipline of the Navy and hazards of their profession many of the seamen must have dreaded the day when their ship would up anchor and carry them away from that wonderful paradise. There was food and drink in plenty, and women so beautiful and friendly that some sailors collected as many as six 'wives' during their visit, and a few became men of property for the first time in their lives.

Discipline became slack, mainly because some of the young officers were too entangled with their own affairs to pay attention to their proper duties, and when Bligh enforced and put right their wrongs he was naturally enough seen as the villain of the act.

Christian, whom Bligh had promoted to acting lieutenant, was no less involved ashore than many of the crew, and was equally loath to face the prospect of another year's voyage in cramped misery and return home after the delights he had found in the islands.

Bligh, however, in his usual methodical and unswerving

manner, had made his plans, and in spite of the hostility from some of those he had been forced to punish, and the non-co-operation from the cantankerous Fryer, made ready to sail. It is worth noting here that when three deserters were recaptured after stealing a ship's boat and a stand of weapons Bligh awarded the minimum punishment. Many captains would have had the men hanged for what was one of the most serious offences in the Navy at that time.

As in most serious happenings, the spark which caused the final explosion was almost trivial.

Twenty-three days after leaving the anchorage Bligh discovered that some of the carefully collected coconuts had been stolen. The nuts were a very important addition to the normal daily diet, but at the time the loss might have been regarded of little importance.

But Bligh had had enough. In spite of repeated warnings his officers had failed to carry out his orders. The missing nuts had gone while an officer had stood his watch nearby, so in a sudden fit of blinding rage Bligh suggested that his officers had stolen the nuts themselves. To jerk them back to the realities of being once more on the high seas he stopped their grog and cut their rations until the nuts were either found or replaced from their own stocks.

Not much, you might think, but it was enough. Next morning the mutiny exploded.

All in all it was a skilfully planned and executed affair. Christian, who had been trusted by Bligh as his previous promotion verifies, had been careful to gather all the ship's troublemakers into one watch, his own, so that when he passed the order to seize the ship it was all over in a matter of minutes. Men who by rank or service were considered to be loyal to the captain were separated and placed under guard, the arms chest opened, and all that there was left to be done to make the mutiny complete was to decide the fate of Bligh and his loyal subordinates.

It is well worth noting at this point that the punishment for mutiny, whether or not any superior officer was killed or wounded in the act, was death. The mutineers had nothing to gain by leaving Bligh and the others alive, and by so doing would only endanger their own lives should he or some of the others reach a port where a search could be instituted. If Bligh had been even half of the tyrant portrayed in films and stories of our century they would have put him to death without any hesitation. It had happened before and was to occur again in other ships, although few of these bloody mutinies have received much attention in recent years.

The mutineers aboard the *Bounty* were content to cast Bligh adrift with the other loyal men, to fend for themselves as best they could, while they returned to the islands and to what they hoped would be a continued sample of paradise. Their thoughts were so full of excitement and danger of their action that they were too dazed perhaps to face reality beyond the next weeks or months.

But one aboard the *Bounty* above all the others kept his head, and that man was Fletcher Christian. He knew Bligh better than anyone, had served with him before and had formed his own impressions of his tremendous stubbornness and competence as a professional seaman. There can be no doubt that on that bright April morning Christian intended Bligh to die. He was not blinded by the excitement of what he and his companions had so far achieved, and knew more than they what still lay ahead. The Navy would not rest until it had run them to ground,

had caught, tried and hanged every man jack of the
mutineers, both as punishment and as a warning to others
in the future. If any man might survive in an open boat he
knew Bligh could, and having reached that decision he
showed both his final disloyalty and his true self perhaps
for the first time in the whole affair. He instructed that the
ship's cutter should be lowered and the men who were to
accompany Bligh to be put aboard at once.

But for the intervention of some of the other mutineers
the story might have ended shortly after that point. It may
never have been told, and the *Bounty*'s fate could have
stayed another sea mystery for all time. For that cutter,
chosen and insisted upon by Christian, was completely
rotten and worm-eaten and totally unfit for use. It would
have foundered almost as soon as it was filled, as every man
aboard the ship was well aware.

Why some of the mutineers went against Christian's
wishes is not completely clear. After all, the boat finally
given to Bligh was not much better, even though it was
sound and well built, and the chances of it surviving were
remote to a point of impossibility. Maybe they thought
that out of sight, out of mind was the best and fairest
policy. Or perhaps they were so confused by the events
which had taken charge of their own lives they no longer
cared for the past and wanted merely to get rid of the
officers and the authority they still represented by their
presence.

Eventually Christian agreed to lower the ship's launch
and again ordered the loyal men to climb down into it.
Apart from Bligh himself there were eighteen others,
mostly warrant and petty officers, and Nelson, the
botanist. The launch was twenty-three feet in length with
a beam of six feet nine inches, and once filled with the

castaways was so low in the sea that there were only seven inches freeboard above water.

After further argument Christian allowed certain additional stores to be thrown down into the boat, but it was little enough. Some sails and cordage, a twenty-eight-gallon cask of water, four empty beakers, 150 pounds of bread, a few pieces of salt pork and some oddments of clothing. As an afterthought a small quantity of wine and rum were also added.

Bligh requested to be allowed some firearms, but this plea was refused. Maybe Christian still believed he might try to retake the ship. But Bligh was already thinking ahead and knew that the hazards facing him and his small company were bad enough without being unarmed as well. They were nine leagues from any sort of land, and the surrounding islands were alive with hostile and dangerous natives.

And when Christian further refused him any charts or a timekeeper, or even the navigational drawings he had made earlier on the voyage, he must have known that his trusted acting lieutenant intended him to perish and all those with him.

Just before the boat was cut adrift the mutineers threw four cutlasses to the wretched men who were looking up at them, as their only protection from attack or from each other.

All Bligh had was a sextant, a few notes and an overwhelming anger and determination to reach safety, if only to see those who had betrayed and stolen his precious *Bounty* tried and hanged for their crime.

Then the line was cast off, and as the boat drifted clear the *Bounty*'s men made sail and headed away in search of their own salvation.

Nothing is recorded of the thoughts in the minds of the castaways as they stood or sat in the small, crowded boat and watched their ship grow smaller and smaller towards the horizon. From Fryer, the master, to the youngest midshipman, the one outstanding sensation must have been total despair.

The seas around them were largely uncharted and unknown, and the distance from any sort of friendly port almost impossible to guess. It was a moment when many could be excused for giving way to complete terror and panic.

We should pause here to examine more closely the sort of men who had been thrown together in the small launch.

Most of them were the ship's professionals, and included the boatswain, gunner, three young midshipmen and the sailmaker. More important, as it was to turn out, there was also William Purcell, the *Bounty*'s carpenter. Like Fryer, the master, he was a difficult and very argumentative person who had fallen out with Bligh almost as soon as the ship had sailed from Spithead. Bligh had had occasion to warn, even punish, him at various times, but Purcell had remained as always unrepentant and tactless. Today we have become used to industrial demarcation disputes, but Purcell must have been one of the first men to start one in the Navy. When the *Bounty* had been at anchor and her seamen had been ashore gathering wood and fresh water the carpenter had refused pointblank to assist the men who were hoisting casks into a longboat. It was not, he hotly declared, the work for a man of his station and experience.

Nevertheless, Purcell was a first-class carpenter, and even managed to cajole the mutineers into allowing him to take his tool-chest with him into the boat. His skill was to prove very valuable in the weeks which followed.

Bligh ordered sail to be set, and without more ado turned the boat towards the nearest island of Tofoa. His past service in these waters with Captain Cook had given him a good idea of what he was against, and he knew the scanty stores available to him and his men were quite insufficient if they were to survive, let alone reach help.

He decided to send some of his men ashore to scavenge for more provisions, coconuts and fresh water and then get under way again for the larger island of Tongataboo. There he hoped to persuade the king, a man named Paulaho, to help him equip the boat for a longer voyage and furnish him with better and more nourishing food for the journey.

In due course they ran the boat on to a shallow beach, and while some of the men went off to look for food, Purcell got to work on the boat's gunwale. By using his scanty stocks of wood and timber he made a narrow screen around the top of the gunwale, heightening the freeboard as best he could to prevent the boat from being swamped once it got into bad weather. Even on the trip to the island they had been kept busy trimming the hull and bailing to prevent it happening, and as yet the sea was running quite low.

They had not been at the island for more than a few hours when some natives approached and settled down to watch the newcomers with obvious interest. Bligh ordered his people to remain close to the boat and was apprehensive as to what the natives intended. But they seemed friendly enough, and were content to remain some distance away.

Eventually, however, one of the natives, a chief of some kind, approached the busy sailors and enquired what Bligh was doing, and, more important, where was his ship?

Bligh was in a quandary. If he told the natives what had happened they might decide to attack, especially as their numbers had grown considerably since the boat had come ashore. He decided to tell a half-truth, that his men were survivors, and that the ship had foundered. It was pointless to tell a complete lie, to say the *Bounty* was close at hand, for a seaman had already reported to Bligh that several powerful-looking canoes were beached in another cove, and their owners would know of any ship in the vicinity.

The natives still remained curious and outwardly friendly, but Bligh grew more and more worried. He had noticed they were well armed and were slowly moving closer to the part of the beach where most of his men were working. Four cutlasses would be less than useless against so many, so under cover of darkness he moved the stores and provisions back into the boat and ordered it to lay off the beach until first light.

The local chief and his growing number of followers were already awake when Bligh walked down to instruct his own men to prepare for a quick retreat. He asked Bligh to seat himself and be his guest. But Bligh observed that several other natives were trying to get between him and his crew and knew then the chief was attempting to seize him as a prisoner.

Ordering his men to cast off, he ran into the sea and jumped into the boat after the rest. The effect was immediate. A hail of stones and jagged rocks crashed down over the boat and several of the occupants were knocked almost senseless. Feverishly they worked at the oars, but as the launch backed clear of the beach a sternline became fouled, and yelling and screaming the natives rushed into the water to complete their victory.

John Norton, the *Bounty*'s second quartermaster, jumped over the gunwale and disregarding the peril to himself waded up the beach to free the line which was still holding the boat fast to the land. Even as he cut it with his knife he was overwhelmed by the horde of natives and torn to pieces before the horrified eyes of his companions.

Pulling with all their strength, the dazed and battered sailors took their boat into deeper water, only to discover they were now being pursued by several fast and powerful canoes. The latter were not only loaded with men but filled with more of the sharp rocks which had been used in the first attack.

The launch was slow and heavy by comparison with the native craft, and soon the sailors were cowering under an onslaught of missiles. They could not close with their enemy, nor could they fight them off, and it seemed that their escape had finally ended.

Bligh tore open the parcel of old clothing in the bottom of the boat and hurled some of it into the water. It was only a faint hope, but it worked. While the canoes stopped to retrieve the floating garments Bligh and his men pulled further out to sea until their attackers were finally lost from view.

Norton's death had made everyone realise just what lay ahead, and what they could expect from now on. He had been a seasoned and popular seaman, but as Bligh wrote dryly in his diary that day, if anyone was to die, Norton was the best choice, since he was the fattest and heaviest in the boat.

The savage attack had caused Bligh to alter his decision

to make for the island of Tongataboo. It seemed likely they would be attacked there also once the natives realised he and his men were unarmed and powerless to summon help. He decided to turn and head for Timor, a Dutch colony some 1,200 leagues away.

He hoped to be able to gather some coconuts at any islands he might pass on the voyage, and replenish his meagre stocks by catching fish or seabirds as the opportunity afforded. But he could afford no chances and set a rigid daily ration of one quarter of a pint of water and one and a half ounces of bread per man. The rum and wine he wisely retained for the first men to fall sick from thirst or exposure.

And so day followed day, and each more wretched than the one before. At night it was bitterly cold, so that they huddled together in the boat, soaked to the skin, bailing or trying to find relief in sleep, while in the daytime they suffered all the agony of a blazing sun and the attendant torture of thirst.

On May 5th they sighted a small island, but camp-fires warned them of the presence of natives, so they sheered off and continued on their way. The following day it was the same, with lush, inviting islands and the threat of attack which forced them to keep moving.

On one occasion two large sailing canoes came out after them and gave chase, but Bligh managed to outdistance them by using his sails in spite of the danger of being swamped.

They were constantly wet and dogged with fatigue. Yet Bligh managed to keep his men from despair, and even found the time to write in his diary of the daily pattern of events and sketched the passing islands with such skill that they were later used by other, more fortunate navigators.

Their first piece of luck came in the shape of a sudden rainstorm. It quenched their raving thirst, and while they lifted their faces and sunburned arms into the deluge they also succeeded in storing a further thirty-four gallons of it for future use.

Bligh had constructed some scales for weighing out the daily rations. By using a pair of coconut shells and some pistol balls for weights he was able to share the scanty stores fairly. This was all-important, for men driven to the extremes of hunger and thirst will soon lose control of their tolerance if they suspect any sort of favouritism or short measure.

They had no luck with their fishing, although a hook had been trailed astern every day for the purpose. So Bligh issued an ounce and a half of pork a day to supplement the rotten bread, and gave a small tot of rum to each man to try to keep up their spirits. To pass the time and to keep their minds away from the nearness of failure he gave lectures on his previous travels, of New Guinea and New Holland, and of the ships he had once served. But inwardly he was getting worried at their appearance. They were looking thinner and took less time to get exhausted, while some were showing real signs of distress.

On May 10th a great storm got up, with thunder and lightning and crashing wave-crests to add to their plight. All night they bailed and fought to stay afloat, and even a tot of rum failed to restore their strength when the daylight came again. Bligh decided to alter course. By using his sextant, his memory and his sailor's sixth sense he calculated that it was time to turn towards the New Hebrides, or where he hoped they were situated, for without charts his dead reckoning and calculations were largely guesswork. He wanted to pass north of the New

Hebrides and then turn further westwards towards New Holland, but with the weather worsening and the fierce currents it was often impossible to plot anything approaching a true position.

Four days later they sighted land which Bligh believed to be the New Hebrides. That night it was pitch dark and rained incessantly, with no sleep for anyone aboard, nor a star to steer by. Bailing and using the oars as well as the sodden sails Bligh fought to drive his little boat closer to the invisible land, knowing that if he failed to make use of the southerly wind there was the real danger of being driven on to New Guinea, which would have meant the end of the voyage, and of their lives. For several days they fought against wind and sea, with great waves breaking over the hull and each man so sick and weary it took all of Bligh's determination and skill to keep them from dropping with fatigue.

They all craved sleep and several were in a truly serious condition, but Bligh could not let them rest. He dared not. They had to sight land soon or he would know that the boat was hopelessly off course and he had been wrong about his earlier position.

By May 25th the wind had dropped and they managed to catch their first seabird, a noddy. Later they also caught a booby, about the size of a duck, and this Bligh divided into eighteen tiny portions, giving the bird's blood to the three weakest men in the hope it would keep them alive.

To Bligh the birds represented more than food. They meant that land was close. Next day they seized another booby and divided it as before, but the blazing sun had returned and more of the men were getting weaker and more despairing.

Bligh watched over them through each endless day, encouraging, threatening and nursing them in his efforts to hold them together. He had sighted some driftwood and floating branches and knew that land was near. It had to be.

In the early morning of the 28th the weary helmsman heard breakers, and when dawn found them Bligh sighted what he knew to be the Great Barrier Reef off the coast of Queensland. All that day they coasted along the great reef, searching for an opening to the calmer, protected water beyond. Eventually they found one, and taking advantage of a south-east wind they sailed through the reef and later that day sighted land.

It was in fact the coastline of Australia, and those in the boat who still had the strength stood up to cheer and weep at what must have seemed like an act of God.

It was a remarkable feat of skill and navigation, and as Bligh made his issue of bread and water he must have felt justly proud of himself and the men who had trusted in his ability to get that far with so little to sustain them.

The main consideration at that moment in time was to find a safe landing place where he could rest his men and deal more comfortably with the sick ones.

Discovering a small rocky island which he estimated to be about 130-foot-high, Bligh had the boat run ashore, and while some of his men scouted around to ensure that no natives were in the vicinity the rest helped and carried their weaker companions into the shelter of the trees.

There were some signs that natives had visited the island, but the old fireplaces were decayed and scattered and it seemed unlikely that anyone had been there for some while.

Putting Purcell and his assistant to work on the boat,

just in case they had to make another speedy exit, Bligh
sent the bulk of his men in search of food. They found some
oysters, and mixed with some pork and a little bread the
cook prepared a stew in a copper pot which one seaman
had fortunately carried with him from the *Bounty*. The
making of a fire was quite a problem until Bligh, ingeni-
ous as usual, used the magnifying glass from his sextant,
the one normally needed to read the tiny divisions on the
instrument, and with the aid of a tinder box found on one
of the men soon got a good blaze going.

Each person received a mug of this doubtful stew, and it
was about this time that Bligh got a hint of more trouble
brewing between himself and Fryer, the master. The latter
complained loudly in front of the men that he considered
the ration too small, even though he, better than most,
should have realised the uncertainties which still lay
ahead. Purcell, as usual, added his grumbles to Fryer's,
and Bligh's temper was not improved when some of the
others appeared in agreement with his old adversaries.

But the stew seemed to put fresh heart into most of
them, and they were soon at work gathering more oysters
as well as fresh water which was in plentiful supply on the
island.

The next day a lookout reported the approach of a
large group of natives and in due course they appeared on
the opposite side of the small bay where the boat was
beached. They were heavily armed, and Bligh decided it
was time to leave.

They sighted more islands to the north-east, but when
they drew closer saw parties of fierce-looking natives
watching their progress from the beaches and decided to
stay well clear. But another island, north and west of the
boat, looked more promising, so Bligh set sail towards it,

7 William Bligh: Captain of the *Bounty*

8 The *Bounty* mutiny. Captain Bligh is cast adrift

9 Rare picture of World War I German U-boat. Large ocean-going type.

and landed there early the following morning. It was a Sunday, and Bligh named it Sunday Island.

They gathered a few coconuts, but upon discovering a large canoe partly hidden in the undergrowth Bligh decided it was too risky to make camp. It was at Sunday Island that his bad feelings with Purcell came to a sudden and explosive head.

He had ordered two parties of men to move in opposite directions to gather food if any was available, and the rest, including the more sickly ones, to stay in the boat. There were murmurings and complaints, mostly from Purcell, who hinted that if the men decided for themselves where they should go Bligh could do nothing about it, as he was alone and outnumbered. Instead of leaping forward to back up his captain, or to seize Purcell bodily and declare him a mutineer, Fryer, the master, added his own complaints to what had fast become a very dangerous situation. Bligh knew that if his authority cracked they were all done for, and to have any hope of survival they had to remain a close-knit team. As he had more than proved already he was certainly the only man in the launch capable of leading them and sustaining them through the next weeks, or longer if need be.

Anyway, Bligh acted in his own particular way by flying into a blazing rage. Cursing Fryer for his disloyalty he snatched up two of the cutlasses and after handing one to Purcell offered to fight him to the death there and then. It is hardly surprising that Purcell did not accept the challenge, instead he humbly asked forgiveness for his outburst. Fryer too lost face and agreed to say no more against Bligh in the future. That was to prove a lie, but nevertheless Bligh's impulsive action made a deep impression on the rest of the men and at no other time did they falter in their trust of his orders or his integrity on their behalf.

Once clear of Sunday Island, Bligh headed westward again, towards the mainland of Australia, and on June 1st beached the boat on one of four small keys. It was, he calculated, about twelve miles from the mainland, which he could clearly discern from the top of a small hill. He named the place Lagoon Key because of its protective reef and sandbars. A comfortable and sheltered mooring place for the launch which was beginning to show almost as many signs of strain as its occupants.

Unfortunately there was no fresh water on the key, but Bligh considered it a suitable place to rest his men and give them another hot meal.

Giving strict instructions to keep the camp-fire under control and low enough as to be invisible from unwanted intruders, Bligh went himself to measure the extent of the key and its relationship with the others close by, sketching them in his worn logbook as he had done throughout the hazardous journey.

Returning a little later he was aghast to see the hillside glowing from a great, blazing fire. He learned that Fryer, in spite of his orders, had insisted in having a camp-fire all of his own, and in so doing had accidentally set the nearby grass and brush well alight.

Bligh was furious. It was bad enough to be let down once more by his cantankerous second-in-command, but he knew too that he had only twelve men left who were fit and still able to fight off an attack.

The short stay at the key was further marred by one more piece of carelessness. A foraging party sent by Bligh to seize a large number of sleeping seabirds nearby returned with only twelve captures, and most of them were very small. The *Bounty*'s butcher, aptly named Lamb, had apparently frightened all the other birds away just as his companions had been about to seize them.

Bligh's anger was getting plenty of fuel, and, as he wrote later in his diary, he gave the fool Lamb 'a good beating'.

Leaving the key they sailed on to the north, following the coastline and watching out for hostile natives. On June 3rd they sighted and closed with another small island, but left almost immediately when they discovered many turtle bones strewn about near the beach, as if a great feast had just taken place. Bligh named it Turtle Island and reluctantly made sail again.

Although he confided his thoughts only with his diary, Bligh was worried. The weather was much worse and he was finding it hard to keep his men in good spirits. The boat was leaking constantly and required bailing most of the time, and he was getting anxious at the condition of some of the other sailors around him.

In spite of their promises, both Fryer and Purcell were grumbling again. It was mostly about the small quantity of food which Bligh rationed each day, even though Fryer was well aware of the tiny portions left in the boat and how long they might be needed to last.

Even so, Bligh managed to keep up with his sketching and noting, and it must be true to say that some of the men found comfort from watching him at work. It could only have given an impression of calm and confidence, although to Bligh's methodical mind it was probably the obvious and practical thing to do.

On and on, amongst reefs and swirling currents, with the bitter cold nights and blazing days to taunt their every mile of progress. They managed to catch another booby on June 6th and shared it between them, keeping the blood for the most needy.

By June 9th things were very bad indeed. The sea had got up and it was impossible for the men to dry themselves or be spared the backbreaking work of bailing as the waves surged over them. One of the older men, Lebogue, was in a very low state, as was the acting surgeon, Ledward, while most of the others were lolling with fatigue and exhaustion.

Bligh gave Lebogue, who was the *Bounty*'s sailmaker, and Ledward some of his tiny stock of wine, and tried to encourage them, although on that day he himself was feeling strangely sick and giddy.

Through the spray and haze Bligh observed what looked like an opening in the mainland and followed the coastline as before, praying that he had not made a mistake in his calculations.

What he did not know until afterwards was that he had traversed the Torres Strait, the most dangerous and treacherous of all Australian navigations, and equal to many of the worst pieces of water in the world.

Battered, sick and half-dazed by sun and sea, Bligh forced his boat on. Somehow he was keeping to his intended plan, averaging 100 to 110 miles a day in spite of everything.

But he was nearly finished. He even admitted to his diary there was little more he could do for his 'brave fellows' who were showing their sufferings so badly. The rations were nearly used up, and there was little left but hope.

It had been a fantastic struggle, and how they had reached that far has been discussed and marvelled at over the years.

But they were not finished. As dawn broke through a low sea-haze Bligh struggled to his feet and stared incredulously across the lolling heads of his men. Through the brightening mist he saw a green and wooded shore rising and hardening and recognised it as the coast of Timor itself. Forty-one days after being cast adrift he had kept his word. He had covered 3,618 miles at an overall average of ninety miles a day, an unbelievable feat of navigation and stubborn courage.

Solemnly they divided a booby into eighteen parts, and while Bligh handed the last of the rum to Lebogue and Ledward they gave silent thanks for their survival and deliverance. For this time there was not a man who had the strength to cheer.

At daylight the next day, after groping their way along the deserted coast, they dropped anchor off a small fort and township called Coupang. It was Sunday, 14th June 1789.

The Dutch governor was astounded with his visitors and did all he could to help with their recovery. Unhappily, David Nelson, the botanist, who had been a tower of strength throughout the voyage and had never complained in spite of the fact that such conditions must have been far worse for a civilian, died of a fever. Thomas Hall, the *Bounty*'s cook, was to follow him some weeks later. Both had been worn out by their exposure and suffering and had nothing left with which to fight on.

While his men rested and recovered Bligh was already busy again. He had purchased and rigged out a small schooner, and named her *Resource*.

On 20th August, with the scarred and listing launch in tow, he set sail with his survivors from Coupang for Batavia, another tale all of its own, to take passage in a larger ship for England.

On March 14th, 1790, Bligh of the *Bounty* landed at Spithead, where the story had all begun.

5

The Silent World

Down over the centuries the many hundreds of types and classes of ships and boats have been as varied and different as the men who faced the sea in them. The need for commercial growth or the expansion of political and imperial conquest have played their full part in ship design and use, because the employment of vessels and sailors have always been forged out of necessity for both good and evil.

If war is said to be the greatest evil, even when the reason for such a conflict may be necessary and justified, it is nevertheless true to say it has usually been the sort of situation from which newer and faster developments in man's fight against the sea have been seen to evolve.

In our own lifetime and the generations of this century, perhaps the one type of craft which has caused more excitement, more alarm and awe, and one which has captured the attention and interest of all, is the submarine.

In two world wars and in other lesser conflicts the underwater exploits of submarines have played paramount, if not totally decisive roles. The object of possessing such a grim weapon in the early days of its production was usually given as a means of defence. To destroy an enemy and so survive oneself. To move in silence like an assassin, strike without warning or mercy and then slink away to await the next victim, such was the purpose, and one which has been expanded, magnified and perfected to the degree it stands today.

Unfortunately, it is only in recent years that other, more realistic uses of the submarine have been visualised, and then again out of sheer necessity.

For beneath the seas and oceans there is another world, vast lands of hitherto untapped resources and wealth, of food and the very requirements to sustain life in an over-crowded and largely undernourished world. As nations expand and standards of living rise, then so too must those resources be enlarged if the weaker and poorer popula-tions are to be given the chance they deserve.

At present we are only scratching at the edges. Mining tunnels run timidly beneath the waters around the coasts, always with the risk of cave-in and seepage. Oil-rigs stand ponderously offshore like gaunt monsters from another planet, and they too have had more than enough accidents and disasters to give room for over-confidence. Drilling for natural gas from the sea-bottom, the uses of television and communication satellites for the furthering of our undersea knowledge, all play their vital part in this, per-haps the greatest of all explorations and conquests for the good and benefit of many in a fast-shrinking world.

But until a submersible vessel can run with maximum safety to any part of the sea-bed, and her crew can actually make contact with the discoveries of such voyages, we are still on the defensive, and the ocean is the victor.

We tend to think more of the submarine 'aces' of the last war, whose skill and tremendous bravery earned respect from every side, or the silent nuclear giants of today, than we do of the men who first attempted to turn a fictional dream into a living, moving possibility.

Jules Verne's *Twenty Thousand Leagues Under The Sea* excited the hearts and minds of many, young and not so young alike, and in today's craft we can see the reality born of that remarkable writer's imagination. But in fact man's attempts to navigate under the seas date from antiquity.

Aristotle, in the fourth century B.C., recorded without any evident surprise or amazement that Alexander the Great used diving bells to carry his men beneath the surface. And during the Renaissance Leonardo da Vinci actually designed a submarine himself. Unhappily, he decided to keep the plans of his work secret. He considered that men would put his ideas to evil uses. One more occasion when he was proved to be right.

The present-day submarine got its first real start as early as 1578, when an Englishman, William Bourne, a mathematician and gunner, put down his ideas and published a work called *Inventions and Devises*.

The craft was to be an enclosed boat, which could be submerged and rowed by oars in the usual way while under the surface. The hull would have a framework above and around the crew, and the whole hull to be covered with waterproofed leather. It was to be submerged by contracting the sides and thereby reducing the volume. A doubtful prospect for the would-be submariners.

His boat was never built, but in 1605 one was launched by a Dutchman, Cornelius van Drebbel, almost exactly similar to William Bourne's own design. There is no surviving record of its performance or operation, but to the Dutchman must go the credit of the first ever workable submarine.

His boat was strengthened by iron bands and covered with well-greased hides to keep it waterproof. Twelve oarsmen sat inside, their oars passing through greased sleeves, but otherwise placed in the same way as in surface craft. The boat was then ballasted until it was nearly submerged, and when the oarsmen began to row the hull was forced below the surface by its own momentum. It must have been a grim experience for all concerned. Van Drebbel demonstrated what his boat could do before no less a person than King James I on the River Thames. The King was very impressed when the small submarine maintained a depth of twelve to fifteen feet for several hours, and it is said that he actually made one trip himself. This royal interest fired van Drebbel to greater efforts and he built an even larger boat on the same design as the first.

A Frenchman called deSon was the next firm contender, and his boat was constructed in a Dutch yard in 1653. It was as ungainly as it was ambitious. It was propelled by a paddlewheel which in turn was driven by clockwork. Once wound, the paddle's motor would run for eight hours, and when you think that all other ships were still being moved by fairly elementary sail-plans, deSon's invention must have seemed like a bombshell.

The inventor was not content merely with his design and product. He claimed that his submarine could 'undertake in one day to destroy a hundred ships, can go from Rotterdam to London and back again in one day, and in six weeks to go to the East Indies, and to run as swift as a bird can fly, no fire, no storm, no bullets, can hinder her unless it please God'.

But the submarine's engine power, aided perhaps by God's displeasure, failed to budge it, and the poor inventor was laughed into oblivion.

Almost a century later, in 1747, a man named Symons launched his own submarine on the River Thames, and amazed the nautical world by submerging it by actually admitting water into the hull. The water was allowed to enter a number of leather bottles, the necks of which were tied as soon as enough had been admitted to submerge the entire hull. To return to the surface Symons squeezed the water from each bottle and then retied the necks once the boat had risen above the danger level. It was slow and awkward, but history had been made. The first submarine ballast tank, on the same principle as today's, had been made and found to be safe.

Others still favoured the more solid forms of ballast, however. In 1773 John Day, a ship's carpenter, built a well-shaped wooden submarine and took it down to a depth of thirty feet and then rose again to the surface. In World War II the periscope depth of most submarines was only thirty feet, so we can appreciate Day's achievement.

His ballast was made up of big rocks, suspended to the boat's keel. When enough had been attached, the hull sank. By depressing a lever inside the hull Day was able to release the ballast and thus allow it to surface again.

If Symons gave us the ballast tank, poor John Day was to show everyone what was, and still is, one of the greatest hazards known to submarines.

On June 20th, 1774, he gave his second ambitious demonstration in Plymouth Sound. Naval experts and many sightseers were there. It was Day's big moment. Rocks were attached to the hull, and very slowly Day took it down to a depth of 132 feet. The great pressure crushed the submarine and its crew to fragments. Another grim lesson had been learned.

It was during the American War of Independence that the real potential of the submarine as a weapon became

apparent. Two Americans, David Bushnell and Robert
Fulton, had thought about making their submarine for
some time. War provided not only the necessity but also
the stimulant. Against a great sea power like Britain, and
cut off from other friendly nations by vast distances over
which the British naval patrols kept a watchful eye, some
sort of balance was needed, and needed quickly.

Bushnell had discovered how to explode gunpowder
under water. The Chinese had learned to do it many years
before, but apart from crude uses the European nations
had made little advance in the matter. The submarine,
which they named the *Turtle*, was like nothing else before
or since. Most submarines have been cigar- or fish-shaped,
whereas *Turtle* was like a large, upright egg. It was made
of steel and was just big enough for a one-man crew, who
was required to work a maze of complicated gears as well
as con the craft towards its objective. The latter, chosen
with great care, was the mass of British shipping in New
York harbour. The *Turtle* could manage some three knots,
and was propelled by a double screw operated by hand,
rather like pedals on a cycle. It had a diving time of
thirty minutes, quite long enough it was thought, and once
against the target a detachable explosive charge was
designed to be screwed into the hull of the enemy, to be
detonated after the little steel egg had got clear.

H.M.S. *Eagle* proved to be the most accessible ship
when the *Turtle* came to make her first attempt. But the
warship had a copper-sheathed hull, then comparatively
rare, and the charge failed to attach itself. *Turtle* was
sighted from the warship's deck, but so great was the
surprise and consternation aboard, that the submarine
was able to get away unharmed. The gunpowder exploded with no effect, but by making contact and getting

away in safety the *Turtle* had more than proved the worth of the new weapon of war. In the later war of 1812 Bushnell had another attempt on a British ship, H.M.S. *Ramillies*, anchored off New London. This time he used a larger version of his design, but again the charge failed to make contact completely, although it did explode and blew a hole in the warship's hull. The attempt to sink a powerful adversary had failed, but the submarine still succeeded in making good an escape.

Robert Fulton had an even more frustrating time with his own submarine designs. He went to England, the old enemy, in 1794, and while putting his mind to other, more rewarding inventions, like spinning machines, a mill for cutting marble and similar industrial ventures, he continued to elaborate on his ideas for the perfect undersea craft. England was at war with France, so Fulton set off across the Channel to try his luck with the new Revolutionary Government. The British Navy had already showed its superior skill, so that France was the obvious choice for the sale and manufacture of a new and devastating weapon which might even the balance.

The trials of his new boat were amazingly successful. More amazing still was the fact that he could not get the French to show a really serious interest. In our lifetime this has often been the case. For if war produces inventions, it rarely seems to produce the minds of authoritative people to appreciate their worth. For several years Fulton hawked his submarine around Europe, but to no avail. When he returned to France in 1800 he sought the attention of Napoleon Bonaparte, a completely different character from the argumentative and suspicious veterans of the first revolutionary government.

Napoleon, a born strategist, saw the possibilities and

gave Fulton the backing he needed, and in 1801 his submarine, the *Nautilus*, was completed.

Nautilus was designed to screw an explosive charge into her target in much the same way as the egg-shaped *Turtle*. There any similarity ended. The new boat was cylindrical and built of copper, and submerged by admitting water into proper tanks within the hull. She carried enough air for her four-man crew to stay alive for three hours, and was lit by candles. Submerged she was driven by hand-operated propellers, but on the surface her crew stepped a folding mast and made sail in the accepted style.

Excitement mounted when a successful attack was carried out against a target ship moored off Brest. More so when it was blown to pieces at the first attempt.

But when he tried his submarine in earnest against the blockading British men-of-war outside Brest, Fulton was dismayed to discover that he could not get near enough to any target. The British ships merely kept on the move and refused to let him near, and loosed off a few cannon balls whenever the *Nautilus* attempted to surface and replenish her air supply.

Napoleon immediately lost interest. To do him justice, he had more than enough troubles already. The British were winning at sea each time the French fleet, usually superior in numbers, poked out from its harbours. A young and daring British admiral, Horatio Nelson, had also emerged to add to his problems, and his lines of communications across Europe had been stretched to the limit.

Had someone listened to Fulton earlier, who knows what might have happened? The Glorious First of June, St Vincent, The Nile, Copenhagen and Trafalgar, to say nothing of many other great British victories, might have been stalemated by the appearance of several, better-equipped boats like *Nautilus*. But wars are not won and lost by the *maybes* and the *if onlys*, and all we do know is that Fulton packed his bags and set off for England for one last chance.

He was lucky to meet William Pitt, the young and quick-thinking Prime Minister, who allowed him to give a demonstration. Again it was successful, the *Nautilus* despatching the brig *Dorothy* off Falmer in a very short time.

But once more the weight of authority was against Fulton. Lord St Vincent opposed the *Nautilus* by saying, 'Pitt was the greatest fool that ever existed to encourage a mode of warfare which those who commanded the seas did not want, and which, if successful, would at once deprive them of it'. Had Nelson been in charge of the Admiralty instead of being constantly at sea with his fleet, it seems likely that Fulton would have got the backing he needed and richly deserved.

Instead he returned to America, disappointed but still determined. He went to the complete limit of his inventive power and produced a new submarine, the *Mute*, driven by a steam engine and capable of carrying a hundred men. During the trials, however, Fulton died, and the *Mute* lay neglected at her moorings until finally she sank and was forgotten.

A Bavarian, Wilhelm Bauer, built two submarines. The first, *Le Plongeur-Marin*, sank in 1851 when on trials off Kiel. The next, *Le Diable-Marin*, drew the attention of the Russian Government, but Czar Alexander II lost interest because of a somewhat embarrassing accident during Bauer's special demonstration. He had taken several musicians aboard, and as they played the Russian National

Anthem and a vast crowd stood watching in silence, the submarine inadvertently dived in the middle of the sacred anthem, leaving the small band spluttering in the water. It was not so comic for Bauer, and in disgrace he returned to Germany.

Another armed conflict, this time the American Civil War, gave submarine design a new chance. It was during this conflict that a submarine was to make the first combat sinking and throw open the door to what followed.

The submarine was the Confederate *Hunley*, and she was the third to be built in an attempt to sway the war against the North.

The first boat, the *Pioneer*, had been lost before anything could be done, and the second was sunk at sea in a sudden storm, so that there was a good deal of scepticism at the worth of continuing building them at all.

But the *Hunley* was finally completed and made ready to show her paces. She had started life as a large iron boiler which had been lengthened and shaped to some thirty-six feet. A propeller was turned from within by eight men and a shaft, and the maximum speed was about four knots. The *Hunley*'s weapon was a torpedo containing ninety pounds of gunpowder which was to be towed behind the submarine on a long line. Once the *Hunley* had dived beneath a target, the torpedo would then be towed on against the ship's side and complete the conquest. It needed iron nerves, and a good deal of luck.

The first trial was successful, but while on passage the *Hunley* was swamped by a passing steamer and sunk. Only one man survived. The hull was raised and a fresh crew trained. Again the *Hunley* carried out a successful trial and practice dive. The next dive took the entire crew to the bottom and their deaths.

Deterred? Not a bit of it. The *Hunley* was raised and fitted with a long spar, like a lance, with an explosive charge of great power on the tip of it. All they had to do was approach the target and prod into it with the spar. Simple.

So with a new crew the *Hunley* set off, and on the night of February 17th, 1864, she confronted the Federal warship *Housatonic*.

The *Hunley* made her attack on the surface and rammed the warship hard with the spar torpedo.

The explosion was heard and felt for many miles around. On the shore, windows were shattered and buildings shook, whilst in the anchorage moored ships rocked and pitched as if in a hurricane. The torpedo had in fact exploded the *Housatonic*'s magazine. The great explosion sank both attacker and victim. All on board the submarine were killed, but only five were lost from the *Housatonic* before she sank. It is ironic to realise that in her brief but violent career the *Hunley* killed about eight times as many sailors of her own side as that of her enemy!

Nevertheless, the *Hunley* had made her mark in history. The shock-wave from that explosion was to go on echoing down the years, and the acceptance of the submarine as a realistic proposition was decided.

In the years which followed many types of submarine appeared on the maritime scene. In 1880 an English clergyman named Garrett invented a steam-powered boat which contained a coal-fired boiler and had a retractable funnel. The Swedes followed with a twin-screw model, but it was in 1886, when two Britons named Ash and Campbell announced the completion of their electric powered submarine, that the next great step forward came about.

The French, and even the Spanish, took to the idea of

10 Control room of a World War I submarine

11 British submarine M–1. One of a pair of large experimental boats built too late for World War I. Mounted, apart from torpedoes, a huge 12in. gun. Sister boat, M–2, had gun replaced by seaplane hangar. Neither was a great success

12 H.M. Submarine *Thetis* after being raised from the bottom, alongside salvage vessel

building a submarine arm to their navies, although the latter decided against it at the last minute. That decision was unfortunate for them, for after the Spanish-American War the famous American admiral, George Dewey, told the Naval Committee of the U.S. House of Representatives that if the Spanish had possessed just two submarines at Manila, 'I could never have held it with the squadron I had. The moral effect—to my mind—is infinitely superior to mines or torpedoes or anything of the kind'.

By the turn of the century the pace had grown hotter. At last the problems of powering submarines had been overcome. Electric storage batteries were installed to run the boats' motors submerged, and petrol, later diesel, engines used to run them on the surface while charging batteries for the next dive.

The British were somewhat reluctant to take part in the race. The Royal Navy was the most powerful in the world. The submarine, therefore, was more likely to be used by a less powerful navy, and seemed more of a threat than a potential weapon. But quite rightly the British public did not share this view, and in 1901 the Navy ordered five submarines for training purposes.

Strangely enough, Germany was almost the last nation to begin creating an undersea force. The German engineer Rudolph Diesel had already invented a suitable surface engine to run on oil instead of the more dangerous petrol, and it was his interest and example as much as anything else which began the start of the U-boat fleet.

The very first U-boat tasted salt water in 1905. She was a mere 236 tons and carried only one torpedo in a firing tube. But the stage was set. There was no longer time to turn back from the inevitable.

The outbreak of World War I still found plenty of

otherwise intelligent and informed people unable to accept that the submarine was anything more than a luxury, a glamorous sideline from the *real* war of battle cruisers and trench fighting.

Those same people, indeed the whole world, were soon shocked out of complacency and into stark reality. On September 14th, 1914, within weeks of the first shot being fired, the U-9 sank three British cruisers off the Belgian coast. Three fine ships and 1,200 officers and men sent to the bottom, almost it seemed in the twinkling of an eye. The U-boat returned unharmed to her base.

Encouraged by that early success the German submarines began an all-out attack on every type of surface shipping. Merchant vessels, cruisers and even a battleship followed in quick succession, and when a U-boat torpedoed the great liner *Lusitania*, killing men, women and children, the world realised just what they had unleashed.

There was not much in the way of defence in those early days. Sentries were posted at ships' guardrails with orders to shoot their rifles at anything which looked like a periscope. Rowing boats patrolled around anchored shipping and dropped grenades if they saw a shadow moving below the surface. Anti-torpedo nets were later fitted to bigger ships, and captains began to paint false bow-waves on their hulls to deceive any watching U-boat commander as to their real speed.

For the submarine commander the problems were also very great. The firing equipment was unsophisticated, and much depended on the commander's eye and brain to assess the range, course and speed of a potential target.

In their small, dripping hulls the submariners worked in extreme discomfort for most of the time. They suffered intense cold, and food which went rotten in the unnatural air almost as soon as it was opened. Water seepage brought the additional terror of chlorine gas from the batteries, and mice were carried to warn of any such escape. Diving and surfacing were always hazardous, and often a submarine would take charge and dive wildly out of control for the bottom, never to rise again.

Then there were the new ethics of sea warfare. If a U-boat commander surfaced to allow the crew of a ship to take to the boats before he sent it to the bottom with a torpedo, he would quite likely find the target to be a Q-ship. These strange vessels, manned and commanded by brave and dedicated sailors, put to sea to act as bait. When a U-boat surfaced and ordered them to stop a dummy crew would appear panic-stricken on deck, take to the boats and row clear with great haste. Encouraged, the U-boat would draw closer, only to see false deck-houses vanish, side flaps fall away, and find themselves peering down the gaping muzzles of several powerful guns manned by the Q-ship's real crew. Even if the U-boat managed to get off the first shot it was often not enough. The Q-ships were crammed to the hatch covers with timber. They were literally floating gun platforms, and several U-boats were despatched in that way. It did not, however, encourage German submariners to rely too much on the ethics of warfare. From then on it was sink on sight.

Sinkings mounted, and so did the efforts to defeat them. Britain was faced with blockade by the U-boats, and that meant starvation. But help was coming. Underwater listening devices, depth-charges and the convoy system began to reverse the terrible toll of merchant shipping, but it was plain to everyone by then that the submarine was a force to be reckoned with. British submarines attacked enemy coastal shipping to good effect, and like their opposite numbers soon found that the strain and constant vigilance were just as brutal for the crews as for any front-line soldier.

The undersea craft had sounded the death knell of the great battle-fleets. The proud columns of giant armoured ships like those which had fought at Jutland and the Dogger Bank would never feel safe again if a single submarine was nearby.

The deeds of courage by submariners on both sides were many and varied. The acts of cruelty and inhumanity by some were also worth remembering. A helpless, unarmed merchant ship. An empty sea. All was peace. Then the telltale line of white foam streaking across the surface and the shattering roar as the torpedo exploded deep in the vessel's bowels. It was so familiar that men grew hardened to it. Men also became afraid, and from that fear came the hatred to hit back with the same lack of mercy which they had once received from a torpedo.

By the Armistice in 1918 both sides had had enough of it. German U-boats had reaped a rich harvest. In the last ten months of the war alone they had sunk 1,103 ships of every type and nationality with a loss of eighty-eight of their own boats. By superior tactics and a better system of escort ships the British had just tipped the balance against them. But the price was already far too high. On the Western Front and in Flanders mud the dead lay in millions. It was the war to end war. Everyone was sure of it, and the very mention of a submarine was enough to fan up a wave of post-war horror and reaction.

But to those who remembered the lesson, who had seen the submarine's work at close quarters, the work was only then beginning. More designs, new power units and larger hulls to withstand great pressures and depths were already being built in half a dozen countries.

Submarines which carried their own aircraft, others driven by steam, and a giant boat which mounted two massive guns in a turret like a surface cruiser, the list seemed unending. As the clouds gathered over Europe once more so the race speeded up. There were accidents and internal explosions. A nation cried sabotage when it was usually some submarine putting to sea long before her design had been properly tested. In June 1939, when H.M.S/M *Thetis* went down on trials with her crew trapped inside and in sight of land, the country demanded better safety measures for those who chanced their lives at every dive.

Once again it was already too late. The Germans marched into Poland, we were at war.

The war at sea was to follow very closely the pattern of the previous conflict as far as submarines were concerned. U-boats ranged the Atlantic and preyed upon the desperately needed convoys. The British boats had to make their attacks closer inshore or in the Mediterranean and Baltic where they were of the most use.

The Battle of the Atlantic, as it came to be known, was fought from first to last with great determination by both sides. New anti-submarine weapons and tactics on the one hand. Homing torpedoes, a breathing tube or snorkel for U-boats to run their diesels while submerged, and finally wolf-pack tactics, used on the other.

There were all sorts of ideas. Midget submarines, little craft with four-man crews, made their appearance and crippled the great battleship *Tirpitz* in her Norwegian harbour. Italian frogmen riding on torpedoes attacked

British battleships in the safety of their anchorages. A U-boat actually penetrated the base at Scapa Flow and sank the battleship *Royal Oak* within weeks of the war's outbreak.

Submarine history was also made when H.M.S/M *Venturer* operating off the Norwegian coast torpedoed and sank a German U-boat while both craft were submerged. It was the first and only time it had happened, and a fore-taste of the killer-submarines of today.

At the end of the war it was apparent that for any future design in undersea craft there would have to be a completely new conception of power and construction. Radar and improved listening devices had made surfacing by day or night to charge batteries a chancy affair, with a real risk of discovery and destruction as the result. Even the snorkel was only a temporary answer, and they often jammed or snapped shut in a heavy sea. The British submarine *Affray* plunged to the bottom with her snorkel fractured taking her whole crew to their deaths.

The Royal Navy came up with what they thought was the answer in the 1950s. Two boats, the *Explorer* and the *Excalibur*, were constructed to run on hydrogen peroxide. It was safe, economic and enabled the boats to work in comfort with little noise and a minimum use of the air supply. When used as 'targets' for surface craft they often moved quite freely amongst the hunters without being detected.

The birth of the nuclear powered submarine made the hydrogen peroxide boats and all else besides into so much history. It was as breathtaking as the change from sail to steam, from paddle-wheel to the screw, from bow and arrow to the automatic rifle.

The use of the nuclear reactor enables such vessels to

remain not only at sea for long periods, but also to stay submerged for weeks, and if necessary months, without seeing daylight or refuelling at any time.

Compare these present-day monsters of 8,000 tons with those tiny, dripping hulls of the First World War and some idea of the speed of advancement can be understood.

They are in effect submarines in the fullest sense of the word. Before, the time submerged was small when compared with surface cruising, charging batteries and so forth, but with the new and reliable nuclear powered engines surface time is reduced to the mere necessity of entering and leaving harbour.

The nuclear boats have gone around the world, and even under the great ice masses at the North Pole completely submerged. These achievements make the earlier tests of endurance seem almost amateur, although to the men who took the chances in those forerunners of under-sea development it was anything but that.

As is often the case, some early achievements in the conventional craft were overshadowed and almost unnoticed because of other events in the world. There was the German submarine U–977, commanded by Heinz Schaeffer, which at the surrender of his country in 1945 went all the way to Argentina to be interned and so avoid the humiliation of being handed over to the enemy. Schaeffer made the record voyage of sixty-six days totally submerged, something unheard of, and still regarded as a real stepping-stone in submarine endurance.

In 1967 the British nuclear submarine *Valiant* covered a minimum of 8,200 miles submerged from England to surface for the first time in the Straits of Malacca. The experimental American boat, *Triton*, made an eighty-four-day passage around the world in which she covered 36,000 miles, although her voyage was in fact interrupted at least once to transfer a sick crewman to another ship.

Greater endurance, longer range and deeper diving depths, the demands seem unending in man's search for underwater perfection. And the cost has been high. In 1963 the U.S. Navy's nuclear submarine *Thresher* plunged out of control to the sea-bed, 220 miles east of Cape Cod, taking 129 submariners and civilian workers to a terrible end. In May 1968 another American nuclear submarine, *Scorpion*, passed a radio message to her home base at Norfolk, Virginia. She was near the Azores, and everything seemed normal. Then there was silence. The greatest sea-air search was begun, including the use of tracking satellites for the first time. Much later the location of the missing submarine was discovered, but there was nothing left of her, nor could she have been reached at such a great depth even if she had survived the last plunge to the bottom. The great pressures at such depths can crush even such a giant like a sardine can, and the problems of rescue are magnified proportionally.

A submarine lying helpless in a great depth of water and still intact must be found quickly so that rescue operations can begin. If the hull cannot be raised then her crew must somehow be got out. The old ideas of men escaping through open hatches and floating to the surface are only useful in shallow depths. Diving bells, miniature submarines and lifting gear, all are cumbersome and complicated. They cannot be everywhere, and while the stricken hull lies on the bottom in the black silence of an ocean, the rescue equipment and the teams of men to work it may be on the opposite side of the world.

Today in America scientists are working on the real

possibility of producing tiny submarines which can not only withstand great pressures, but are also capable of being flown direct to the location of a wreck within hours. Working in conjunction with surface and salvage craft, they will be able to attach themselves to the sunken hull like sucker fish and so extract the men from their steel prison. The task of producing such methods of rescue is enormous, but at least now we know what we are up against. Further, we know that without a reliable solution the ocean bed will remain unconquered as before. And already the underwater traffic is growing at an impressive rate. Quite apart from the world's fleets of combat vessels, men are at last venturing into the commercial uses of submarines as a real and important step to undersea development.

In World War I the Germans produced a massive submarine named *Deutschland* entirely for commercial purposes. Cut off from a neutral America by the British naval blockade, Germany used the giant boat to carry on with her Atlantic trade and so gather vital cargoes of food and war supplies without hindrance from above. She made a great impression in American ports and proved that such craft could be used successfully, although with limited types of cargo. America's entry into the war put paid to the *Deutschland*'s peaceful use, however, and she was converted into a war vessel.

In the Second World War British submarines were frequently used to carry food and necessary supplies to Malta, when that embattled island was cut off from help by German and Italian air attacks.

The Germans, too, used fuel-carrying submarines for the first time. Large boats were constructed to transport diesel oil and other seagoing requirements for the Atlantic

U-boats, and so cut down the time normally required for the latter in harbour. The supply submarines would move from rendezvous to rendezvous and await their various broods to make contact. Then, fuel pipes would be connected, and while oil was pumped across, other much needed supplies of food, soap, spare parts, as well as morale-raising letters from home were passed over in rubber dinghies or waterproof containers.

Today the study and planning of possible submarine merchant ships is nearing reality. There are many advantages over the surface craft. They are untroubled by turbulence and surface storms. A submarine has the advantage of high-speed operations and does not generate bow waves as does the surface ship. An ordinary merchant ship cruising at a comfortable speed will use a good part of her power merely to combat the pressure of those bow waves, whereas the submarine moves unhindered. The faster she moves, the more profitable is her ratio of commercial usage.

The opening up of Alaska as a rich and highly competitive source of oil supply will surely go down as the real incentive to recent submarine design. Surface oil tankers are hampered by pack ice, some have even been stopped altogether when trying to reach their ports of loading. A submarine tanker, however, will be able to traverse the Northwest Passage or the Arctic Ocean under the ice, carrying as much as 170,000 tons of Alaskan crude oil from the North Slope direct to the eastern coast of the U.S.A.

And what tankers they will be. The initial design shows a veritable goliath of submarines. Nine hundred feet long, and displacing over a quarter of a million tons, nuclear-powered and equipped with all the sonar, radar and navigational aids necessary to keep her clear of surface ice and underwater hazards, she will be unparalleled in maritime history.

To gain some idea of her proposed size, if she were to be stood on end next to the Empire State Building her bow would reach the upper level of the great building's observation deck.

Even Jules Verne never contemplated such a vessel, and there is no reason why the growth of ideas and designs should stop here.

Another plan already being considered is that of a submarine 'tugboat', one to haul a train of submerged inflatable or rigid liquid cargo carriers to any part of the globe without refuelling. The carriers could be switched or detached in any port, rather like a freight train, without the time-wasting necessity of unloading the whole cargo before putting to sea once again.

At the moment it is the prohibitive expense of producing a nuclear powered submarine which still deters the world's shipping companies from plunging into the race. Only the bulk cargoes, like crude oil, and the necessity to overcome the real problems of ice-blocked passage have made possible the world's first tanker design.

No doubt there will soon be more advances in the field of nuclear technology, and the present difficulties of competitive and realistic constructions will be overcome.

When you think of those first-ever submarines and remember they were nearly all rejected as useless or unusable by men who were too short-sighted and too set in their own restricted lives to see what the future had in store, it gives hope for another advance, and this time for peaceful purposes, in our lifetime.

And we must not forget all those other submarines and

their intrepid—if sometimes too ambitious—crews who have got us this far with their own efforts.

In our computerised and ordered world we can look back at David Bushnell's steel egg, *Turtle*, and afford to smile as well as admire him for his determination and courage. We should also pause and think of the years stretching out ahead. Perhaps one day, and maybe not too far off, others will look at our own advances and give what might be a condescending smile.

By then, whole communities may be working on the sea-bed, reaping a rich living which until now has been denied to us all.

6

The Oarsmen

Mention the Atlantic to a professional sailor in any quarter of the world and it is likely that you will hear little good of it. For of all the great oceans it still remains in many ways the most dangerous and the most treacherous. Its vast expanse lies like a record of history itself, of the ships and men who have challenged its latent power from choice or out of hard necessity.

The bottom of the Atlantic is littered with every type of craft, for this ocean is not particular who or what it destroys. To discover far off lands in the Americas, to carry trade down to the Caribbean or to wage war, men have again and again challenged the Atlantic, often at the expense of their own lives.

It has seen them all come and go. Proud square riggers and clipper ships, the rusty tramp steamer and plush liner, the desperate convoy or prowling U-boat, and lastly but by no means least those brave, reckless few who have taken the ocean's waiting challenge as a sport, a game of chance.

For to men who take nothing but an oared boat, the strength of their arms and the stubborn determination of pioneers, the Atlantic has become the ultimate, the great contest between sea and human. They know that once clear of the land they have only themselves and their courage to rely on. A small boat hardly records anything on a ship's radar screen, and even a searching aircraft equipped with every modern detection device can miss finding such a craft when passing within a few miles of it.

On the face of it the chance of survival, let alone rowing a small boat the three thousand odd miles of hostile ocean seem remote, yet men still take on the challenge, and some of them succeed. Curiously enough, most of the successful Atlantic rowers have been amateurs, that is to say they were not men who normally earned their living at sea. It is also worth noting that in wartime, particularly in the Second World War when the Battle of the Atlantic raged back and forth with mounting ferocity and cost during nearly six years of combat, there were few recorded instances of professional seamen reaching safety in whatever craft remaining at their disposal after a shipwreck.

Often these men survived many days, even weeks, at the mercy of the Atlantic in all weathers, to be found sometimes by searching escort ships or passing convoys, and it is a wonder that so many of them lived through it. But it is rare to read of any who sailed or rowed their lifeboats in either direction to reach safety under their own power. Perhaps the shock of losing their ships and of seeing friends die while they survived left them with little else but their courage and a will to hold on until help arrived. The torpedo and bomb, the mine and the nameless explosion which tore ships apart in those terrible times were enough to strip away a man's initiative beyond the small spark of hope.

Those who take up the Atlantic as a sporting challenge do it with their eyes wide open. They count the chances on either side, weigh the cost and then go about it with the same quiet resolution as a mountaineer or racing driver.

If the 1960s are remembered for little else, they will mark the decade of challenge, when several such oarsmen took to the ocean with varying degrees of success or tragedy.

It seems strange that it took so long for the Atlantic to attract attention in this way, especially as the first successful crossing was made as far back as 1896. Maybe the turn of the century brought so many inventions and new ideas that the sportsmen and adventurers were too dazzled to see the obvious. The aircraft and the fast sail-boat, improved methods of navigation and a widening scope of man's ability seem to have put the Atlantic in the background until more recent times.

In 1896 when the two Norwegian oyster fishermen, Harbo and Samuelson, started on their lonely voyage most people wrote them off as madmen, doomed to failure and death. In an open eighteen foot boat they set off from New York with none of the modern refinements which we now take for granted. No dehydrated foods or compressed survival rations. No radio to summon aid or to tell them of approaching storms, and their protective clothing was little more than that which they used in their daily work.

But the Norwegians not only succeeded in making the crossing in the fantastic time of fifty-five days, but went on into the English Channel and down the River Seine before allowing themselves to be satisfied. For the last miles of their incredible journey they donned bowler hats, so it would appear that they not only had courage, but also retained a good sense of humour to the end.

Like the successful oarsmen who were to follow them, Harbo and Samuelson had a great understanding and knowledge, not only of what they were undertaking, but just as important, of each other.

But what of the man who attempts the crossing on his own? He has no one to encourage him when the going gets difficult, nobody to set an example if his own ability is failing when most needed. Yet in 1969 two such crossings were made, one from east to west, and the other in the opposite direction.

On a July day Mrs Maggie Lavell was walking along the coast road above a beach near Blacksod Bay on the west coast of north Eire. All at once she saw a haggard, soaking figure climbing up from the beach and staggering towards her.

The stranger said calmly, 'I've just rowed the Atlantic. Can you take me to a telephone?'

He was Trooper Tom McClean, a twenty-six-year-old British soldier, and he had become the first man to row the Atlantic alone from west to east. He was serving with the Special Air Service Regiment, the same one that produced the two Atlantic oarsmen three years earlier, Captain J. Ridgway and Sergeant C. Blyth.

But unlike some of the other crossings, this was a very personal affair in more ways than one.

As a senior officer of his regiment commented afterwards, 'It was a completely solo effort. All the regiment has done is to give him its blessing and paid leave to make the voyage.'

The other remarkable fact was that Trooper McClean was completely inexperienced as an oarsman before making his attempt to cross over 3,000 miles of ocean. A brave man indeed.

To take the best advantage of favourable currents for the first part of his crossing McClean made his starting point at St John's, Newfoundland, and chose as his boat a twenty foot Yorkshire dory which he named *Super Silver*.

Two of the essential factors in his success were physical fitness and stamina, both of which are almost taken for granted in a regiment like the S.A.S. They were to stand him in good stead through the gruelling weeks which lay ahead of him on his solitary voyage.

For McClean it was no slapdash, thoughtless decision. He had thought about his attempt for two years, and was quite determined to be the first man to do a solo crossing from west to east. He knew his own strength and his limitations, and planned every detail accordingly. Eighty days was the span he allowed himself for the task, not much when you realise that he already knew Ridgway and Blyth had taken ninety-one days from Cape Cod to Ireland. And there had been two of them.

Very much an individualist, McClean chose his rations to suit his own tastes, rather than to accept the normal offerings made by experienced sailors. During his Army service he had been in Malaysia, and while there had acquired a great liking for curry. So curry became the major part of his rations, which was not only to his liking but also proved easy to stow in a small space and not too difficult to prepare under the more favourable conditions.

Unfortunately McClean was plagued by anything but good weather and had to endure an average of one gale a week which pitched the little *Super Silver* about like a piece of driftwood. It was a case of sheer physical strength to keep the boat from being hurled on its beam ends, and says much for its clean construction and design.

The captain of a Finnish steamship who sighted McClean during his voyage reported the boat as being like 'a child's toy waiting to be picked up with one grab of the hand'.

Rowing fifteen hours a day and snatching sleep when

he could in between, McClean fought the Atlantic almost with his bare hands. He had stormy weather for days on end, but took comfort from the fact that the winds which sent the icy spray dashing into his face were blowing him towards Ireland and his goal. Much to his surprise he was never seasick at any time, but it seems likely he was kept too busy for that.

At every hour of the day and night he was very aware of his complete isolation. If he was swept overboard or received a crippling injury he was helpless. If his oars were smashed or the boat stove in he was at the mercy of the sea. Nothing could save him.

It was during one of his brief catnaps that he came to realise just how thin the margin of survival really was.

On July 17th, after two months alone and unaided, he awoke from a doze to find himself struggling in water. For one more dreadful moment he imagined he had been swept over the gunwale but then realised that the boat had been swamped by a great wave and was actually awash. It was a bad situation and a time when any lesser man might have lost his nerve completely.

As he struggled to find out the extent of the danger the boat yawed and staggered beneath him, and sometimes it was completely under the surface, kept afloat only by its buoyancy tanks. Bailing was out of the question and time was too short for half measures.

Without more hesitation McClean leapt into the sea and tilted the boat back and forth to free the hull from the main bulk of water. It took great strength and a lot of determination but after several hours he managed to clear most of the crippling weight from the dory and only then hauled himself back aboard to complete the task inside.

Unknown to McClean, he was then only 250 miles from Ireland.

After a short rest and a well earned meal he continued at the oars, and on the morning of July 27th sighted the land over his shoulder, his reward for all that had gone before.

Even in the last few yards to the shore he still had to fight. The one and a half ton *Super Silver*, almost within reach of a beach, smashed itself dangerously on to some submerged rocks. Being alone and with his back turned towards the bows McClean had not seen them, and once again had to leap into the sea. Using his remarkable strength he heaved the boat on to the top of a flat rock to save it from being pounded to fragments, and having made sure it was secure began to wade up the beach.

Wet through, tired and bruised McClean climbed up to the coast road where he met Mrs Lavell on her walk. He had succeeded in his ambition with only one miscalculation. His voyage from Newfoundland to Co. Mayo in northern Eire had only taken him seventy-two days! A remarkable record for a truly remarkable oarsman.

Strangely enough, McClean was only beaten by nine days in being the first ever solo oarsman to cross the Atlantic in either direction. John Fairfax in *Britannia* reached the Florida coast after leaving the Canary Islands for his east-west crossing some six months earlier. Fairfax and McClean attempted and achieved the same goal in opposite directions even though their personalities and methods were as different and as distant as the two shorelines.

Fairfax was probably the most unorthodox oarsman of all time. He survived the many weeks at sea by drawing his strength from it. He had already thrown much of his stock of food overboard, preferring to live off the sea by catching fish, and even finding the time to fight with and catch powerful sharks while he filmed himself in the process.

From these examples of Atlantic oarsmen the reader might judge that all one needs to cross the Atlantic is determination, courage and a well-found boat. These things are of course necessary, but as always where the sea in general and the Atlantic in particular is concerned the oarsman needs a good deal of luck too.

The crossing takes so long that any change of weather can bring instant disaster. An oared boat can only take the most limited precautions to avoid an approaching storm, even when forewarned by radio. Whereas a steamship or boat under sail can run before the sea and wind and can find shelter if given half a chance.

It merely needs one of the Atlantic's changes of mood, a sudden vicious squall or freak pattern of waves to transform a brave adventure into a catastrophe.

In May 1966 two men, David Johnstone and John Hoare, in their little fifteen-and-a-half-foot-long *Puffin* started off on the west to east crossing under their own power.

On the afternoon of October 14th the lookouts of H.M.C.S. *Chaudière* on passage from Nova Scotia to the Mediterranean sighted what appeared to be a piece of floating wreckage. Closing to investigate, the warship's crew realised that the object was a small upturned hull, bobbing in a lazy swell, encrusted with barnacles and half submerged. It was *Puffin*.

The capsized boat was hauled against the warship's side, and while naval frogmen slipped hastily beneath the water to make sure there was no survivor or body still trapped inside the hull, other seamen began to gather the remains, the last available clues of the disaster. The *Puffin* was heavily weighted down by marine growth and barnacles, but inside the tiny cabin the sailors discovered cameras, charts, sodden clothing and food, even the radio equipment still in place. A frayed and severed lifeline brought the searchers to the conclusion that the tragedy had started and ended when it had parted and one or both men had been thrown into the sea.

Only when the drained out wreck and its pathetic remains were safely hoisted on to the *Chaudière*'s deck was the final discovery made, one which was to prevent the *Puffin* from joining the ocean's list of unsolved mysteries. It was the carefully written log of the voyage from Norfolk in Virginia which had started 145 days earlier. Smeared and salt-stained, it was slowly dried and taken to the captain's cabin to await a full examination.

To consider and weigh the circumstances which finally led to the *Puffin*'s disaster and the loss of her two man crew it is necessary to go back to the beginning, when the prospect of an Atlantic crossing had gone beyond a mere dream. In the later stages the attempt had developed into a race, for it was well known that the two intrepid paratroopers, Ridgway and Blyth, were also about to start on their own crossing in *English Rose III*.

Neither Johnstone nor Hoare were experienced sailors or oarsmen, and they went into the matter of boat design and construction with much care, calling only on those who were greatly respected in that field. *Puffin* was built by W. A. Souter and Son (Cowes) Limited, and designed by the famous Colin Mudie. She was of surf-boat design, 15 ft. 6 in. long by 5 ft. 6 in. beam with a weight of some 700 pounds. Fully loaded she weighed one and a quarter tons. Aft there was a small shelter to enable the man off watch to sleep in comfort, with one more bunk for days when the weather made rowing impossible.

One of the most important factors of the design was that *Puffin* was the type of boat which would not turn over.

The equipment was of the best. From the six pairs of oars to the carefully selected stocks of food, the diet sheets and the sea water desalination tablets to supplement the 1,000 pounds of fresh water, all was hand-picked under the advice of experts.

Perhaps not everything was done to allow for the prevailing winds and currents in the North Atlantic, but apart from their complete lack of experience both oarsmen viewed their chances of success with growing confidence.

The voyage to England should have taken fifty days provided nothing unexpected happened. Both oarsmen were physically fit, and their boat and equipment were of the highest quality. And yet, after being at sea for over a hundred days she had actually accomplished only half her planned journey, and was found capsized into the bargain.

The faded handwritten log was to answer some of the many questions which were to be asked about the disaster. But not all of them.

How could such a well-designed boat capsize? Was she even the right sort of craft for such a crossing? And did the total inexperience of the two men outweigh all other advantages?

One thing became quite clear. At no time did either Johnstone or Hoare show any sign of weakening in their courage or determination, even after they had passed their time limit by many days. They could have turned back without shame, but they kept going, cooped up in their tiny tossing world, facing gale after gale, seasickness and hunger, and finally their own unhappy end.

The weather during the first days of the voyage was no help at all. Adverse winds, thick fog and uncomfortable choppy seas made any sort of real progress impossible. On the eleventh day they fixed their position with the aid of two passing trawlers and discovered they were still only forty-two miles east south-east of Cape Henry. But they kept up their spirits and discussed the possibility of Ridgway and Blyth making an early attempt to overtake them.

They did not appear to view the early setbacks as a warning or any sort of reflection of their own ability. Rather as a 'settling down' period while they got used to their cramped life and the business of steering and rowing in all weathers. Occasionally they sighted passing ships, including an American submarine. Most of them offered help which was always politely declined. Only their ability to supply accurate fixes of the *Puffin*'s true position were accepted with immediate thanks.

But on the seventeenth day at sea they closed with a deep laden steamship, the *Orient City*, and after ascertaining their position, which unfortunately put them back thirty miles from their own calculations, decided to accept some beer, cigarettes and a few cans of meat to break the monotony of their own diet.

There is no doubt that the strain of fighting the wretched weather conditions and the growing realisation of their tremendous task were beginning to take their toll. Several times they were almost run down by large ships in the darkness, and once had a curious whale dashing to within a few yards of their small boat. The supply of fresh water was growing stale, and even though they were able to replenish some of the stock during a rainstorm it did little for their morale.

It was the continuous but confined activity which was really getting them down. Rowing and endeavouring to eat their meals in impossible conditions, washing or trying to snatch a few hours' rest while the boisterous lift and roll of the boat made each effort painful and taxing.

And as they consumed their stocks of food and water so the *Puffin* rode higher in the sea and made handling very difficult. On the 2nd July, after forty-three days on the Atlantic, Johnstone wrote of his worries in his log. They were short of everything. Of food, water and paraffin, even of batteries, and they had not set eyes on a ship since the 9th June. And they were on the main shipping lanes, so their loneliness must have seemed both unfair and frightening.

Then two days later they sighted a freighter, but after being hailed by an officer on her bridge they were astounded to see the ship increase speed again and resume her course. Both men were dismayed but still hoped that the ship would turn back to them, and watched it until it vanished into the sea mist for good.

Two more days and they made contact with a fine looking yacht which was taking part in a race to Copenhagen. The yachtsmen gave them their estimated position and offered food and fresh water. After promising to report *Puffin*'s whereabouts they clapped on sail and waved the two oarsmen farewell. It was only a small contact in a great ocean, but it made up in some ways for the freighter's surly dismissal of their presence and needs.

By day sixty-one of the voyage the *Puffin*'s food locker presented something like a final warning. Most of the nourishing rations were gone and there was paraffin for cooking for only four more days.

Overhead the big air liners droned back and forth with their comfortable passengers quite unaware of the plight of two men far below. Fog made an additional hazard as well as lessening their chance of sighting a ship when they required help.

And when the fog cleared they were faced again and again with adverse winds which made rowing all the harder. Even when the oars were lifted between strokes they could feel the boat losing way, and were constantly depressed by the realisation that if they rested they would be blown westwards once more.

The depression mounted when they sighted another ship, for even though they lit a flare and the vessel actually steamed to within one and a half miles of them it did not appear to see them and passed by without reducing speed.

This was to happen again and again, with ships passing so close that they could see their upperworks and markings without much difficulty.

But on July 27th it did seem as if their luck had at last made a change for the better. Instead of soaking fog or blustery gales trying to throw them back the way they had just come, the sun came out hot and bright and the sea changed its grey face to that of a flat, placid calm. To make it a perfect day, and just as they prepared to start a fresh effort at the oars, they sighted a tanker bearing down on them. She was named *Silverbeach*, and within minutes of making contact had slowed down and altered course to allow *Puffin* to get alongside. They too were short of rations, but nevertheless sent down ample supplies of fresh cheese, butter, fruit, corned beef and cigarettes. The tanker's captain was also able to give them an exact position so that past miscalculations could be put to rights.

The oarsmen also asked the whereabouts of their rival and competitor, Captain Ridgway in *English Rose III*, but the tanker's crew had no news of him.

Refusing payment for the supplies the tanker's captain wished them good luck, and with the crew lining the guardrail to wave and cheer his ship returned to the original course to the westward.

That meeting and the sight of another ship on the horizon did much for *Puffin's* morale, and with a good meal for the first time in days they took to the oars with fresh determination and better spirits than they had known for weeks.

Two days later the fog came down again and visibility fell to fifty yards. Between rowing and resting both Johnstone and Hoare tried their luck at fishing with some success, and later enjoyed eating their catch after stowing some of the better morsels away for future use.

All seemed to be going well. The fog dispersed before a friendly following wind, and with the added power behind them they had the *Puffin* bowling along at a better speed than ever before. It was difficult to keep the stern on to the following sea, especially when the wind continued to rise until it had reached a Force 8. This difficulty in handling the boat with a strong wind astern meant that they had to alter course at right angles on more than one occasion, so that the seemingly good speed and distance they had accomplished was eventually shown to be less encouraging. For instance, nine days after their meeting with the tanker *Silverbeach* they had covered an additional 146 miles and no more. They were using too many stores and too much energy for the end result, and from comments in *Puffin*'s log it does seem as if they were becoming too dependent on meeting vessels in the main shipping lanes in order to supplement their food locker.

And so the voyage continued. Oily calms and raging gales, with the oarsmen fighting like mad to keep the wildly bucking boat under command. Even with the sea anchor out it was hard to stop the boat from broaching to in the great, battering cross seas which loomed above *Puffin*'s hull like grey cliffs.

Several ships passed apparently without seeing them or their frantic signals, but one cannot be too harsh on deep-sea sailors because of this. A small boat or any such object is hard to see in a tossing wilderness of whitecaps and steep-sided rollers. And who would expect anyone in his right mind to be rowing a small boat in mid-Atlantic? As is often the case, ships' lookouts see what they expect to see and not necessarily what is there. Hours of peering at an empty, tossing expanse of ocean, a matter of routine rather than urgency, and the lookout's vision cannot be relied on too much, any more than the swinging impartial eye of the radar.

Yet their luck had still not deserted them entirely. On 11th August, their eighty-third day at sea, they sighted one more ship on the horizon. She proved to be an American Coastguard vessel, and as soon as they manœuvred alongside it did seem as if their troubles, as far as supplies were concerned, were over for some time to come. The Americans, with all the usual generosity and kindness of naval men, showered them with food and stores of every sort, refusing payment and insisting that the two oarsmen could stay with their ship, alongside or on board, just as long as they needed to regain their strength and composure.

It made a great change from all the disappointments and being bypassed by other ships, and it was with great reluctance that they had to cast off and continue on their way once more.

They had both faced up to the grim fact that they could never reach their goal in the time expected. In fact, by the 16th August they calculated they would not reach the other side of the Atlantic for another sixty days, a longer period than they had planned for the whole voyage!

But in spite of the bitter truth they kept to their routine as well as they could. Much of their valuable rowing time was lost because of adverse easterly winds, when there was little they could do but ride to a sea anchor and consume some of the food given them by the American Coast-guard.

A week later the written log showed that their morale was again on the ebb. The weather was worse, with blustery squalls and soaking spray to add to their general discomfort. The motion left them little peace. Up and down, this way and that, with the tiny hull pitching amidst the waves like a cork.

It was becoming increasingly difficult to keep the boat end on to the sea. This was partly due to her top hamper, and also caused by the obvious strain and weariness of both oarsmen.

In the tug of war between wind and current, sea and human strength, the *Puffin* was losing way badly and being thrust further and further to the south, so that the average daily gain in mileage was pitifully and dangerously little.

It was obvious at that time it was no longer a matter of beating the other boat in the race, but merely a question of staying alive. The game had changed, and once more the Atlantic was putting on the pressure.

Like her crew, the *Puffin* was showing signs of heavy strain. The hull was working badly, and most of the carefully selected gear was either faulty or totally useless. On the 1st September they sighted the navigation lights of a passing ship, but, as their own signal lamp was out of order, had to stand and watch her pass them, ignorant of their desperate situation.

The next day both men had a discussion in an effort to place where the fault of their predicament lay. Food was very low, and no matter how hard they tried they were making such a poor daily average it was becoming obvious that the United Kingdom was beyond their reach.

Johnstone wrote in his log that day: 'But where are the ships?' It was like a cry from the heart.

Then they lost an oar overboard and it took more vital time and strength to get it back, losing a hard won minimum of thirty yards to do so.

Some corned beef and three biscuits were Johnstone's meal that night as he sat and contemplated the cruel fate which had brought him and his friend so far, and it seemed no farther.

Johnstone wrote of sighting three aircraft overhead, and of a small bird which he could not recognise. The comments seem vague and disjointed after the factual and carefully worded reports of earlier days, and he made no comments on their progress.

The last line read merely: 'No rowing because of NNW wind, Force 2.'

Between that final entry and the moment when the Canadian warship *Chaudière* found the capsized boat on 14th October nothing is known for sure. But there can be little doubt that the actual cause of *Puffin*'s disaster was Hurricane FAITH, which according to all calculations would have been in her vicinity around 3rd or 4th of September.

Whether the two oarsmen could have survived even without the additional hazard of a hurricane is still open to conjecture, but the great storm would certainly have sealed the fate of a boat which had proved so hard to control in anything but reasonable conditions.

The steamship *Ocean Monarch* had already reported sighting a floating wreck four weeks earlier but had not stopped to examine it. It might be argued that even supposing the wreck was not in fact the *Puffin* the steamship should have made some effort to close with it and investigate. An earlier discovery might have held out some hope of one if not both men surviving. Now we shall never know, for the Atlantic rarely reveals its secrets.

With all the comfort of hindsight it is easy to find flaws in the *Puffin*'s plan to conquer the ocean under oars. Inexperience and too little time allotted to get to know the equipment and instruments. A lack of understanding of the monumental task they had undertaken, as well as the boat itself, which was really designed for experts rather than raw amateurs.

It now seems that the *Puffin* should certainly have turned back once the oarsmen realised the hopeless lack of progress in the first four weeks. They still had the strength and the time to select another more suitable starting point, as had already been suggested to them, and their obvious bravery was beyond doubt.

As the weeks dragged on they became too dependent on sighting and contacting ships for obtaining additional food and navigational information, and this must have lessened their own personal reliance and confidence as time ran out for them.

It was a sad twist of fate that their rivals actually made their successful crossing in three months, arriving off the Galway coast of West Ireland on September 3rd, the very day that Johnstone made his last entry in his log.

Four men, two boats and one ocean, yet what a world of difference seemed to have decided the fate of one crew while bringing well deserved acclaim to the other.

There can be little doubt that whereas Captain John Ridgway and Sergeant Chay Blyth in *English Rose III* faced the same hazards as *Puffin*, their hard training and strong self-discipline made all the difference between success and tragedy.

Of *Puffin*'s seaworthiness there can be no doubt, but to keep her stable and steady in the rough seas she experienced it was necessary to replace her used stores with fresh ballast, i.e. sea-water carefully admitted to her bilges. This was obviously not done correctly. Also, the boat was equipped with external buoyancy bags to prevent her capsizing. That they were not fitted or used throughout the voyage is proved by photographs taken before the voyage and from a passing ship during it. This inadequate ballasting would not only leave *Puffin* difficult to handle but would make the likelihood of being overturned a real possibility.

David Johnstone and John Hoare failed in their attempt to cross the Atlantic and gave their lives in making it. But their endeavour and the remaining evidence of the *Puffin*'s log will be a help to those who follow, and their courage will be long remembered.

It would certainly seem that no amount of suffering and danger will ever deter others from making the crossing, no matter now unorthodox or doubtful the methods employed.

On March 10th, 1970, a fifty-one-year-old British house painter, Sidney Genders, succeeded in rowing the Atlantic from east to west, the first man actually to do so from England to the other side. He made his landfall in Antigua in the West Indies 143 days after leaving Cornwall in a twenty-foot-long plywood boat. Hardly the sort of craft most of us might have chosen under such gruelling circumstance.

Experts were further confounded to discover that Genders' long pull was completed under the most abnormal conditions. He used an ordinary school atlas to plan his course, with nothing more for his navigation than a sextant and a wristwatch! His training, he admitted, was carried out on a Birmingham reservoir with none of the refinements normally expected for such a challenge.

He ran short of fresh water, and on one occasion he was struck in the night by a passing ship. But he bailed out his little boat and continued on his way, accompanied for much of his journey by a huge shark. When the shark finally left him alone Genders appears to have been quite sad. As he said afterwards, 'He was really very friendly.'

Perhaps the very impudence of Genders' solitary voyage was too much for the Atlantic. It is hardly surprising.

13 Control room of World War II 'T' Class submarine. The author at the periscope

14 Trooper Tom McClean. First man to row Atlantic single-handed from West to East. Shown in his boat, *Super Silver,* on arrival at Blacksod Bay, Eire

15 Atlantic rowers Captain John Ridgway and Sergeant Chay Blyth in their 20ft. boat *English Rose III* after their crossing

7

For Those in Peril

Around the various and in many cases treacherous shores of the British Isles, at any time of any day or night, a signal flare or distress rocket, a telephone message from a casual observer, or the plaintive Mayday call from the stricken ship herself, can send the men of the lifeboat service running to their craft.

The worse the weather and the more dangerous the coast then the more likely that these volunteer lifeboatmen will be needed, and needed desperately in the shortest time. Most seamen will say that a storm is not too dangerous provided a ship has plenty of sea-room, either to run, or to turn into the teeth of it and ride it out until it has blown over. But lifeboats are required to go to the very places where there is no such room. To a jagged, rocky coast where some helpless vessel may be jammed between the iron-hard fangs and is being torn apart with every crashing breaker. Other ships have been wrecked on treacherous sandbars, where attempting to go alongside in a lifeboat is made even more risky by the danger of being hurled against the larger vessel and smashed in pieces.

Yet as I said earlier, these men are all volunteers, and would have it no other way. The other countries of the

world with many hundreds of miles of coastline to watch
and protect also have their lifeboat services, whose deeds
have often been no less daring than those of our own men.
But it is worth noting that the American service is not only
financed by the state, but is an integral part of the U.S.
Coastguard. Likewise in Russia it is state controlled and
financed, as it is in most other countries to some degree or
another.

Of all the world's sea powers only Britain, Germany and
Holland rely solely on the voluntary contributions of their
people and the unwavering courage of unpaid crews to
provide services whose records are quite unbeaten.

A vast number of our lifeboat crews are made up from
the many and scattered fishing populations from one end
of the British Isles to the other. Men who daily take to the
sea in small boats, who need their local knowledge and
hard-won skill to fetch a living from the coastal waters
where the faster, more powerful trawlers and drifters cannot penetrate. Originally, the forefathers of these men
went further afield in their open boats or in the once
familiar fishing smacks with their stout hulls and tan-
coloured sails. But the steam trawlers with their fast
passages and greedy nets soon put paid to the more
leisurely manner of work, and within a few years the small
harbours around our shores were filled with deserted and
neglected smacks, while their owners were thrown on the
beach without work and deprived of the only life they
knew. Villages shrank, tiny harbours became silted up and
derelict, and many of the menfolk went inland, or sought
work in the deep-sea ships which had in turn destroyed
them.

Yet at no time did these men falter when a rocket
shattered the silence of a storm-tossed night, or a messen-

ger ran breathlessly to some isolated fishing village to tell of one more victim on the rocks or driving ashore with all hope gone.

The lifeboat crewmen hand down their places in their boats from father to son with a pride which is totally unshakable, and in many cases there are several men of the same family in one boat. In one recent disaster practically every man of working age was killed from one village when the lifeboat turned turtle and grounded in a terrible gale while trying to save others' lives from a stranded wreck.

There is the typical case of 1901 when a ship got into difficulties in a storm on the notorious Barber Sands off Caister. As the crew of the local lifeboat threw on their oilskins and tumbled into their craft they were watched anxiously by one James Haylett, a man nearly eighty years of age who had once been the lifeboat's second coxswain. He had an even closer link with the boat that day. The coxswain and one of the hands were his own sons, another, Charles Knight, was his son-in-law, following the closely guarded tradition of their voluntary and humane service. Old James Haylett was also aware that a more recent addition to the crew was his young grandson.

The storm raged violently and the people on the beach prepared to receive the stranded vessel's survivors and waited with their usual patience watching the sea as it surged along the shore.

But when the lifeboat did return it was being driven helplessly ashore amidst some of the worst waves the villagers had ever witnessed. They fought with all their skill, having only oars to pit against the storm's mounting fury, but nothing could be done. Horrified, old James Haylett saw her strike and turn over in a welter of spray, and he was one of the first, in spite of his great age, to wade into the icy water to attempt a rescue.

Only three men survived from the lifeboat's crew that terrible day. Of the nine who perished, two were old James Haylett's sons. In the village several homes were left entirely without their breadwinners.

But James Haylett was to be the one to put the thoughts of all the rest into words in such a manner that they are still remembered.

At the inquest on the drowned lifeboatmen the presiding coroner who knew little of such matters suggested that perhaps the boat had been making for the safety of the harbour when she struck, her mission being too difficult.

The old ex-second coxswain squared his shoulders and said gruffly: 'No, sir. Caister men never turn back.' Nor did they.

The present-day system of lifeboats and sea-rescue services around the many types of coastline is a far cry from those early oared craft which were little better than open whalers. But now, as then, the daily service available to every ship, regardless of her flag or national beliefs, is fraught with dangers. Dangers which make an annual toll of brave men's lives and leave so many families without a complete future.

The first real lifeboats in the accepted sense of the meaning did not really come about until the eighteenth century. In those hard times there were many hazards to be faced by merchant ships as they beat up the English Channel or ran desperately before an Atlantic gale in search of shelter. Some ships were at sea for many months and some did not return to their British ports for several years on end. So it was not surprising that the available shore beacons and safety lights were quickly seen as suitable snares to trap such vessels and lure them on to the rocks, where their survivors could be slaughtered and their rich cargoes whisked away by the men known and feared as wreckers.

One can imagine without much difficulty the lonely barque thrashing past some deadly spur of Cornish headland, the helmsman and lookouts clinging to the pitching hull while they strained their eyes through the spray and darkness looking for that precious beacon which would tell them they were making a correct landfall, that they were almost home. Then, through the darkness the faint, flashing light, and the ship's master would order the yards braced round, the helm put over to run the last few miles to safety and a secure anchorage.

All at once the light vanishes, and before their horrified eyes they see the long broken line of breakers. With the wind in their sails and no room left to wear ship and run for open water they are done for. As they lift and strike, grind forward on to the rocks amidst a nightmare of falling masts and spars, torn canvas and snapping rigging, they see and understand what horror still lies ahead. Many such ships were lost to the wreckers, their crews murdered, their deep holds ransacked and the contents sold for great profit to unscrupulous merchants in distant towns and cities. The forerunners of the big-time bandits and receivers of stolen property we are plagued with today.

So until the larger towns and ports could band together and provide some protection for their would-be lifesavers it was the skill and cunning of a ship's captain which saved him and his vessel, rather than any sort of systematic lifeboat service.

But it could not go on unheeded by the powerful men

who depended on ships arriving intact and fully loaded. Just the loss of one large sailing vessel could smash a business and ruin a merchant, and many came to realise that the saving of life and the salvage and safety of ships in distress was not merely humane. It was profitable.

Out of many ideas and schemes came one solid foundation. The first real lifeboat was built as early as 1784 by a London coach-builder named Lionel Lukin. It was in fact a small yawl and not built for saving life. But Lukin worked on it with the one overwhelming idea that to be of any use at all it must be virtually unsinkable.

To obtain this end he inserted airtight tanks throughout the hull, and strengthened the frames against the real danger of being stove in when colliding or going alongside a disabled vessel.

And, like the whaleboat, it was found the best results could be obtained by having a hull which was pointed at either end, so that the dangers of being overwhelmed by a following sea or 'pooped' could be reduced to a minimum.

His ideas were to attract plenty of attention, but it was not until 1789 that anyone took any really practical steps to make the birth of the lifeboat a reality.

In 1789 at Newcastle a group of influential gentlemen called 'The Gentlemen of the Lawe House' in their meeting place overlooking the mouth of the River Tyne got together to decide the best way to encourage a designer, or several designers, to produce the right plan for a lifeboat, one which was capable of withstanding anything which bad weather in their neighbourhood could throw at it. A prize of two guineas was offered for the best design.

The response was amazingly quick and produced some lively results, not all of which were considered even seaworthy.

However, from a design drawn by a William Would-have, one which incorporated several ideas put forward by other interested gentlemen, a lifeboat named aptly enough *The Original* was constructed by the famous ship-builder Henry Greathead. The design and the finished boat were an immediate success, and *The Original* remained in regular commission until 1830, a long life for any craft. She managed to save many hundreds of lives during her service and was proof, if proof was still required, that lifeboats could and did save life and valuable cargo. She ended her years by being dashed to pieces while attempting to increase her proud record, but by that time she was no longer alone, and already other, more ambitious plans were being studied and put into effect.

It was found, for instance, that many lives were lost at sea because of the wasted time it took for the lifeboat to reach the victim and begin rescue operations. This is quite understandable. A horseman perhaps carried the message from the coastguard to the nearest fishing village where a lifeboat was located. A call had to be sent out to the crew members who were at home rather than earning their living at sea. More time was lost while the lifeboat was launched, usually on log rollers with every man, woman and child putting a shoulder to the hull to speed it into the water.

And still the coxswain had to reach the wreck, often in bad visibility and foul weather. Under oars and in rough seas the lifeboatmen were usually dead-beat by the time they hove alongside their helpless victim, and many good lives were lost because of this.

In 1807 that same Lionel Lukin who had experimented with his yawl and buoyancy tins found part of the answer.

A lifeboat which could not only be pulled under oars but also sailed, thus cutting down the time wasted in the useless distance between base and wreck and leaving the crew fit and ready to deal with whatever was needed.

Lukin's boat was to be the true forerunner of all lifeboat designs, and was the one from which the later famous Norfolk and Suffolk boats were taken.

By 1842 there were many lifeboats scattered around the coasts, of varying design and bound together only by the loyalty and bravery of their volunteer crews.

It was in that year, when there were some thirty-nine boats in service, that the Royal National Lifeboat Institution was founded and some sort of overall organisation was begun.

New leadership brought fresh ideas. A rocket-firing gun was introduced to carry a line between craft, or from a stranded ship to the top of a cliff so that a man could be carried ashore by cradle, or as it was later designed, a breeches buoy. And all the while, as the country's seaborne trade grew, so did the casualties. Reefs, sandbars and collisions. Bad navigation, storms or shifting cargo. Fires, engine failure in the new age of steam or sheer carelessness kept the lifeboats busy from Scotland to the tip of Cornwall.

However, the first excitement which the general public showed at the foundation of the R.N.L.I. was fast giving way to disinterest. There was trouble abroad, the home industry was suffering strife and disputes, troopships left Southampton weekly to fight unknown wars in every quarter of a sprawling British Empire, upon which the sun never set. Those who lived away from the sea soon lost interest in a handful of lifeboatmen. And those who earned their living afloat merely thanked God they had been spared whenever news of a wreck and a gallant rescue reached the more violent headlines of the daily press.

It took a small incident only to bring the country back in support of a service which, like others of its unselfish nature, had all but been forgotten. The memory of that incident has never faded, and the R.N.L.I.'s place in our daily lives is assured.

Today, each time that the North Sunderland lifeboat puts to sea on her errand of mercy, her name, or more precisely the name of the one young girl who rocked a nation's conscience, goes with her. The name is Grace Darling.

Off the busy Northumbrian coast and guarding the Farne Island group are two lighthouses, the Farne and the Longstone. The islands today are a bird sanctuary, but the surrounding waters are as treacherous as they were in the nineteenth century when the original Longstone light-house was constructed in 1826. Some years earlier there had been another lighthouse erected to protect the island group, and that had been known as the Brownsman. It was old-fashioned and ineffective in extremely bad weather, and it was something of a relief for its keeper when the newer and more efficient Longstone was finally completed.

Like the lifeboat crews, those who manned the light-houses around the coasts were often family concerns, father to son, with each growing generation taking the strange, spartan existence for granted. Robert Darling was the keeper of the Brownsman light, so it was only right and just that his son William should succeed him and eventu-ally take over the new post at Longstone. As usual the keeper was paid for his duties attending to the light and watching over and reporting on passing shipping, but un-like today his family lived with him, assisting in running the daily affairs of their isolated home. Keepers' families often found that they were working much harder voluntarily than if they had received a proper wage. Such is the case with volunteers even today.

Bad weather made housekeeping complicated for the women in the family, and it was difficult to plan far enough ahead and prepare for every eventuality. There were few systems of relief in those days, so that keepers were rarely able to take time off with their families. Someone was always needed close by the light. To watch and be ready, no matter how calm the sea might appear.

In September 1838 William Darling was attending to his duties, all alone but for his young daughter Grace, a girl of twenty-two. The weather was bad and a heavy sea was running, and he knew that his son, who had gone to the mainland, would not be able to return to help him if assistance became necessary.

But William Darling had no reason to worry unduly. He was used to bad gales and leaping seas around his lonely pinnacle, and it was not the first time he had been alone.

Young Grace Darling visited her father at his observation post at the top of the lighthouse, and as they both watched the spray bursting against the tower and surrounding catwalk they saw a darker, firmer shape thrashing through the waves, a ship, but far closer than would be expected under the prevailing conditions.

She was in fact the sailing paddle-steamer *Forfarshire*, on passage from Hull to Dundee with a total of sixty-three people aboard.

Unbeknown to the Darlings, the *Forfarshire*'s master was already in difficulties, having bad engine trouble and an extreme loss of power when it was most needed. With such a sea running and a strong gale as well it was difficult to spread any more canvas aloft, and the master, Captain Humble, decided to run closer inshore and take advantage of whatever shelter he could find to get him past the Farne Islands.

In addition to his other troubles, Captain Humble's slow progress was further challenged by a change of wind. It had previously been blowing strongly from a south-easterly direction, but in those critical hours as he was beating past the nearest land in fading daylight it backed to the northward and mounted to a fierce gale. Aboard ship the situation was bad, with seas breaking right over the deck and bridge, and the frightened passengers crouching together behind battened saloon doors or below in their cabins. Had they known how close they were to disaster they would have been even more terrified.

The *Forfarshire* had in fact been driven slightly off course, not much, but when added to the hazard of being so close inshore it was more than enough. As she plunged and staggered amongst the islands, with her seamen fighting to restrain the sodden sails and whipping rigging, she lifted to one great roller and her helm went over. Before anything could be done she struck savagely upon the Harker Rocks, slewed broadside and struck again, harder than before. Almost at once she began to break up.

Poor visibility, the very fierceness of the storm, hid the ship's plight from the two guardians of the Longstone light, and as the wind howled and the seas lifted crazily above the listing wreck it was a wonder that anyone had remained alive.

The majority of the cabin passengers had been killed when the ship had first struck the rocks. Some were crushed in the broken hull, others swept overboard to be

drowned in the raging waters around them. Captain
Humble and his wife had been among the first to die, so
that his leadership and knowledge were denied the rest
when they were most needed.

Of the whole crew and passenger list only thirteen had
managed to climb or fall from the wreck to take refuge on
the rocks. Some imagined it was the mainland, others
were so badly injured and maimed by their escape from
the wreck that they were beyond understanding anything.

During the night, while the sea swept jubilantly over
the pitiful survivors, others began to give up the one-sided
struggle. A mother clung to her two surviving children
until she could hold them no longer. By dawn they had
both gone. Two other adults were also to die before first
light arrived to show the nine dazed and battered survivors still clinging to their slippery and precarious holds.

William Darling and his daughter saw the scene as it
was that morning the 7th September like something from
a nightmare. A few pieces of the *Forfarshire* showed like
broken teeth through the great, white-capped waves, and
against the backdrop of spray and rocks they saw the few
huddled shapes of those who still remained alive.

The keeper had no way of informing the mainland of
the tragedy, nor was there any hope of help reaching the
rocks in time to save the remaining lives.

He had only his own small boat, a coble, and without
hesitation he decided to make his bid to rescue them. His
son was ashore, so his daughter Grace took his place.
Neither questioned or reasoned with the other. It was a
family affair. What was expected.

But once outside their massively built lighthouse what
a sight confronted them. Great crashing waves all around,
against which their tiny boat seemed like a walnut shell.

They climbed aboard, and with William Darling at the oars headed into the teeth of the gale. Tossed about, lifted to a crest only to be dropped like a stone into a trough, they were all but swamped several times. And the closer they drew to the rocks the greater became the danger of being smashed against them before any sort of rescue had been achieved.

As they pitched alongside the rocks where the ship had gone aground it soon became evident that it would take more than one journey even with so few survivors. Quite naturally, too, some of the wretched people clinging to the sea-washed rocks were in no mood to take second place when it came to a chance of survival, no matter how frail the Darlings' coble appeared.

Keeper William Darling manœuvred the boat between the rocks and then sprang ashore to take charge, leaving his young daughter not only to control the oars, but to restrain the little hull from being dashed to fragments.

Five survivors, including the woman who had lost her children, and an injured man, were eventually hustled on board, and the coble started back towards the Long-stone.

It was harder that time as the hull was so overloaded, and several waves nearly succeeded in swamping it before it was a few yards from the rocks.

But they managed to reach the foot of the lighthouse, and without further delay turned to head back for the remaining four men. Fortunately, the Darlings were assisted this time by two of the *Forfarshire*'s crew, both seamen, but their achievement was none the less a magnificent piece of courage and self-sacrifice.

Within an hour of the rescue the Harker Rocks lifeboat arrived on the scene, having been called out by an observer on the mainland some time earlier. Even the lifeboat had great difficulty in surviving the storm's efforts to hurl her across the rocks, so that the Darling's tiny coble must have had a charmed life.

It is worth mentioning that among the regular lifeboat's crew was William Brooks Darling, Grace's brother. And so the family pattern was again complete.

Immediately following the loss of the *Forfarshire* there was such a legal uproar about the causes, the whys and wherefores of the wreck, that the Darlings' part in the rescue, and particularly that of Grace, passed almost unnoticed.

It fell to *The Times*, almost two weeks later, to refresh the public memory and to bring home the true worth of those who daily risk their lives at sea so that others may live.

The famous newspaper asked whether there was ever a single occasion in fact or fiction 'of female heroism to compare for one moment with this?'.

Poor Grace, she did not understand what was happening. She had done what she had considered her duty. After all, she asked herself, who else was there to go to the aid of the stricken survivors on the rocks?

But the shaken public would have none of it. Famous portrait artists pleaded for the honour of putting her youthful good looks on canvas. She was portrayed on stage and in poetry. Even alleged locks of her long hair were sold up and down the country as souvenirs of her outstanding courage. Pleasure steamers were chartered, and filled, to do nothing more than pass as close as was safe to the Longstone so that the passengers could stare in wonder and so share some of that proud incident amongst themselves. Grace Darling was as close to the present-day celebrity as was possible under the austere circumstances of her calling.

Her father was proud of her, but did not approve of such carryings-on. His written report in the Longstone's log at the time was formal to a point of brevity. He finished it by saying briefly, '... and nine others [survivors] held on by the wreck and were rescued by the Darlings'. A quote almost as rare as the actual deed.

Grace Darling's bravery shook the country out of its complacency and money poured in for the upkeep and construction of the lifeboats and the welfare of those bereaved in the fight against the sea's inbuilt cruelty.

But she did not live to see it. Three years after the *Forfarshire*'s loss Grace died of tuberculosis, in those days almost always a fatal disease. She was then only twenty-six years of age.

And now, when the North Sunderland lifeboat puts to sea, motor powered and equipped with every modern device, and still with a crew of volunteers, the name of that quiet, modest girl goes with her. There could be no finer tribute.

Lifeboat design did not change much until after 1849, and this was again brought about by disaster. In the December of that year the hard-worked crew of the South Shields boat were called out to aid the brig *Betsy* which had been wrecked during a sudden squall not far from the land. The lifeboat got into difficulties during the rescue attempt, and before the crew could prevent the hull from broaching to it capsized. Out of a company of twenty-four, only four lifeboatmen survived. The public was horrified and angered. So many had donated funds and support that questions were asked as to the proper use of both money and leadership. The Duke of Northumberland who had become the Lifeboat Institution's second president, acted without delay. He offered a prize of 100 guineas for the best modern design for a boat which would not only be buoyant like the earlier models, but also self-righting in anything but completely sub-normal conditions.

The plans and ideas poured in from every corner of the land and from other countries beside. It fell to James Beeching of Great Yarmouth to submit the right design, and it was his boat which was to be the foundation of those to follow for many years afterwards.

Better systems of communications were introduced so that if necessary more than one boat could be sent to aid a wreck, but at the same time ensuring that all sea areas remained covered by other craft.

The use of power instead of oars and sails made a great deal of difference in the speed of assistance given, but the risks and the chances of death and injury remained ever present. But there was never a shortage of volunteers, and by the time the Second World War had broken out the R.N.L.I. had a record to be proud of. By that time the Institution had saved close on 65,000 lives, a rough average of eleven a week for 112 years of service. As someone wrote at the time, if 65,000 men, the population of an average town, passed a given point, and you had to shake hands with each and every one of them, it would take you over twenty hours!

The safety of ships, the protection of cargoes and the removal of local hazards, all fell to the lot of the lifeboat service, but at the outbreak of war they were to face demands and perils on an unforeseen scale.

Over the years and even during the Great War of 1914–18 the role and the position of lifeboats had been clearly

16 Artist's impression of the new 48ft. 6in. Oakley self-righting lifeboat making for blazing North Sea rig. Drawn by Wilf Hardy

17 Beach launching of lifeboat on the south-east coast

18 The Carss Re King

respected by both sides. But even when individual commanders wished to retain their control over the new weapons at their disposal it was not always possible in the war which was to engulf almost every civilised country in the world. Magnetic mines and aerial bombs of enormous size and destructive power, close-packed convoys in unlighted channels, and scattered wrecks of every type and condition made the lifeboatmen's lives more demanding than ever before.

Oil tankers ablaze from stem to stern, their lethal cargo spilling out over the sea's surface to set that alight, too, still had to be faced and grappled with. For tankers, like all ships, carried seamen, and their lives were of paramount importance.

Vessels loaded down with ammunition, abandoned after being bombed or shelled, had to be boarded. They had to be made safe or towed to an area where their deadly load would not destroy other shipping or endanger life. The lifeboat crews who did such work were not allowed to think of the risk to themselves. It was their job. They got on with it.

Even the anchored light-vessels were not spared. Helpless and vulnerable on their fixed stations they became ready targets for marauding aircraft, and their unarmed crews were bombed and machine-gunned without mercy. There was no sense in such cruelty either, for the light-vessels were as much help to enemy U-boats as they were to our own shipping.

But even the bravery of the light-vessels' men and the ready assistance of the lifeboat crews after an attack could not keep pace with the new dimension of war at sea. The *Nore* light-vessel was the last to remain on her station after her consorts had either been attacked or towed to harbour.

In 1943 she, too, was towed away and her station marked only by a lighted buoy. A reflection on man's inhumanity towards a humane service.

During the great seaborne evacuation of British and Allied servicemen from the Dunkirk beaches the lifeboats were very much in evidence. Back and forth across the English Channel they ferried their exhausted cargoes of soldiers, regardless of air attack and anything which the enemy could throw at them.

The Margate and Ramsgate lifeboats, manned entirely by their own volunteer crews, carried back a total of 3,400 men, and when you pause to consider how small these boats were the figure becomes all the more staggering. In those desperate days at Dunkirk the lifeboats and warships, pleasure launches and tugs, fishing craft and just about anything which would stay afloat, lifted off a grand total of 338,226 men, the greatest rescue of all time.

The Hythe lifeboat was not so lucky. At Dunkirk her bravery and hard work were not enough. She did not return with the others.

Again and again the boats were called on to dash to the aid of ships in distress, or airmen shot down in the sea and awaiting rescue.

They did not hesitate, even though a large proportion of the airmen they were called upon to save were from enemy planes, perhaps even some of the ones who had helped to kill their unarmed comrades. But their creed was clear. They were there to save life and to serve the people of every nation, in peace or war. So the rescue work went on as before.

There was the case of the small, six-ship convoy which ran aground on the Haisborough Sands off the Norfolk coast. It was 1941 and the coast thereabouts was dangerous enough without the strong gale which had suddenly arisen.

Four lifeboats put off into the storm, from Lowestoft, Gorleston, Cromer and Sheringham. The Cromer boat was of course commanded by Henry Blogg, the most famous and the greatest loved of all lifeboat coxswains. One hundred and nineteen men were rescued from those helpless ships, and out of that total number, eighty-eight were saved by Coxswain Blogg's own boat.

In fact, throughout the Second World War the lifeboats saved a total of 6,376 lives, which in no way includes those rescued at Dunkirk. All those men, and quite apart from the countless other duties and calls which they were required to handle.

There were so many deeds, so many acts of bravery in the worst weather and against active enemy opposition that it would be impossible to record them, even in a whole book.

If, since the war, the lifeboats have been spared the dangers of bombs and shellfire, they have found no shortage of fresh demands upon their time and skills.

The vessels on the high seas today are more complex and for the most part far larger than those which went before. Time and economy are everything, for like the clipper ship fought a losing battle with steam, so too surface vessels today must pit their efficiency against the growing importance of air transport and travel.

The Middle East wars closed, even if temporarily, the Suez Canal. That meant the tankers carrying the great cargoes of oil to an industrialised Europe and Scandinavia had to make the long haul around the Cape of Good Hope rather than the swift passage through the canal.

Oil is the blood of industry, so it did not take long for

fresh thinking to change the look and size of the oil tanker to suit the emergency. Fifty thousand tons, 80,000, 200,000 or even 300,000, there seems no limit to the size of these new, mammoth tankers. They will never be able to use the Suez Canal, whatever happens, nor will they want to. Size, tonnage, crew economy . . . they are the ship owner's dream.

But all ships, large or small, have to draw close to land sooner or later. And should disaster overtake these giant carriers, it too is magnified proportionally. It has been said that every type of craft ever built has been destroyed sooner or later. From the dugout canoe to the ocean liner, from a collier brig to a nuclear submarine; none has been too great or too proud to go under.

Lifeboat crews now have to accept that commerce has made such hazards enormous by any standards. Giant tankers take several miles to stop once they are under way. In open water they are supreme, but in close channels and approaching bays and harbours they can become part of a new menace. Collision and fire, oil pollution and internal explosion, all are enlarged and magnified out of all proportion, and the risk to those who go to their aid is also heightened.

So too, a more prosperous way of life has provided the leisure time and money for many more people to get away to sea in their own craft. Yachts, motor cruisers and sailing dinghies, hardly a week passes during the finer weather without news of the lifeboats being sent out to rescue some would-be Chichester or Rose from disaster, or more likely, from himself.

More skills and new equipment are thrown into the battle to preserve life at sea. Radar and long-range radio. Stronger boats and the ready co-operation with other forces such as the air-sea rescue launches and helicopters of both Navy and Air Force.

But when it comes right down to it, it all depends on those familiar blue and white hulls with their oilskinned crews getting to sea without delay. Being where they are needed, and seen to be there by those in distress, and when all else seems lost.

Ordinary men, fishermen, and from other walks of life, who give their skill and often their lives for the benefit of others.

Only recently the Fraserborough lifeboat *Duchess of Kent* capsized in the North Sea and all but one of her crew died. The war has never stopped for the R.N.L.I. Nor will it as long as ships move on the seas and men are brave enough to think of others before themselves.

8

Survival

Over the centuries, as man has fought one battle after another with the sea in all its moods, from the freezing misery of the Denmark Strait to the hurricanes in the South Pacific, it has become more difficult to pick out a few examples to symbolise this endless struggle.

Sailors have been prepared to face the sea's anger in all manner of craft, mostly because their ships have become familiar to their own needs, like extensions of their own weakness and strength. How much worse then is that recurring nightmare when the ship herself, through fault or circumstances, is lost and her crew or passengers are left to find survival on their own.

Listening to seafarers off watch, in the deceptive safety of messdeck or wardroom, it is hard to believe that men once threatened by this, the greatest hazard of all, will still earn their living afloat, knowing that during the next hour or next year it may be their turn.

The two examples of shipwreck I have chosen are different, and as far apart from one another as I could find. Heroism and horror mark them as two of the most outstanding sea tragedies still discussed and remembered, even though both occurred in another century. Neither played any part in history, nor were on the edge of great events, yet both displayed the extreme limits of courage and endurance, of ignorance and brutality, which are part of the sea's own history.

The first story is that of the British troopship *Birkenhead* which foundered off the South African coast in 1852. There has probably been no incident in maritime records which has had a more lasting and profound effect on the conduct, bearing and bravery of men at sea, and which has been a yardstick for subsequent behaviour in similar circumstances.

In 1852 Britain was involved with widespread native uprisings along the frontier of Cape Colony, and the fierce, well-disciplined Kaffir tribesmen were proving more difficult to subdue than had been first thought.

The *Birkenhead*, a paddle-wheeled steamship, after collecting a full complement of military reinforcements set off for the Cape from England at her best speed. She carried more than 600 persons, including twenty women and children, the latter mostly dependents of some of the troops.

The ship was further burdened with horses, supply waggons and several tons of stores and equipment, and her captain was in no doubt as to the importance of his cargo and the speed required to make a fast passage.

Perhaps the ship's captain carried the need for speed too much in his mind, something which may well have overruled his normal reserve and sailor's caution. Trying to cut the duration of the voyage as much as possible he ran closer inshore than usual, and in the early hours of the morning of February 26th the *Birkenhead* struck a great submerged shoulder of reefs just a mile from land.

As was always the case in those times the ship had just her own resources to call on. Before radio to summon aid,

or any kind of communication which might have been
able to call for help, she was at the mercy of the sea. To
make it even worse, the surrounding waters were known
to be alive with sharks, and had there been any sort of
panic the story of the *Birkenhead* might never have been
known at all.

Within a quarter of an hour of striking the reef the
complete bow section tore itself away, carrying with it
some of the passengers and crew who were still trapped in
the darkness below decks. The rest of the broken hull
remained afloat for only another ten minutes, but it is
what happened during that time that made the *Birkenhead*'s name last down the years.

Her captain, Robert Salmond, caught asleep in his
cabin at the time of the disaster, ran on deck to take
charge and stem any panic which presented itself. The
horses, terrified and breaking free from their temporary
stalls, were driven overboard in order to save the passengers from being trampled underfoot as they ran dazedly
about the listing decks. Unfortunately the horses attracted
a school of sharks, and the sea around the ship was soon
red with blood as they slashed in to the attack.

As often happened, some of the ship's lifeboats could not
be lowered because of the increasing list, and the total of
those available was reduced to three when the funnel
collapsed and smashed one boat and davits to pieces.
Three boats, which even optimistically could carry no
more than eighty persons out of the hundreds aboard.

The officer in charge of the troops was a Major Seton of
the 74th Highlanders. In those terrible, vital seconds both
he and the ship's captain knew there was only one thing
to be done. The next order to be shouted above the sounds
of rending wood and metal and the cries of terrified

passengers was to become a lasting pattern of behaviour
in shipwrecks ever since.

'Women and children first!'

As the young drummer boy kept up a steady tattoo, his
legs braced against the growing list, the troops fell in
quietly and without any show of panic. Some were in their
night-clothes, others, like Major Seton, had managed to
throw on their scarlet uniforms before taking their positions with their allotted sections and officers.

They probably looked more pathetic than gallant, but
there can be no questioning their courage.

Without delay the women and children were bustled
into the available boats, although some had to be torn
bodily from their soldier husbands. It must have been a
heartwrenching spectacle for the troops who remained in
their ranks, watching in silence as the ship settled deeper
in the water beneath them.

Including those who were crammed into the boats or
managed to float their way ashore on pieces of wreckage
without being killed by sharks, a total of 210 persons from
the *Birkenhead* finally reached dry land. Not one woman or
child was lost.

A young officer of the 73rd Regiment who did survive,
later wrote of his experience: 'It is hard to describe the
sensation of oppression removed from one's mind on
knowing the utterly helpless part of the ship's living cargo
had been deposited in comparative safety. Thank God it
can seldom be said that Englishmen have left women and
children to perish and saved their own lives.'

The bearing and courage of the men left aboard the
wreck and who perished when the ship took her last dive
gives proof to that officer's words.

For after the boats had been pulled clear Captain

Salmond told the troops that they were then free to jump overboard and if possible swim to the boats, or do what they could to save themselves.

Major Seton saw at once that it was a wrong instruction. The boats were already overloaded and very low in the water. Any sort of additional weight caused by his men clinging to the gunwales would undo all the work so far accomplished.

He passed the order, 'Stand fast!' All but three soldiers obeyed him. The latter broke from the ranks and jumped overboard to try and save themselves, but the remainder stood as before, knowing what was expected of them.

It was this moving moment in history which inspired Rudyard Kipling to write: 'But to stand an' be still to the *Birken'ead* drill is a damned tough bullet to chew.'

Major Seton walked slowly up and down in front of his men, speaking, it is reported, with little outward emotion. He shook hands with some of his subordinates, and when a young officer said fervently that they might meet again on the shore Seton said calmly, 'I do not think we shall. I cannot swim a stroke.'

Then as the *Birkenhead* rolled over and plunged to the bottom, the scarlet ranks finally broke and the troops made a last effort to reach safety. Most were drowned and a few killed by sharks within sight of the shore.

There have been many cases when the order to 'Stand Fast!' has meant that some shall die so that others may survive. It is doubtful, however, if there was ever a more rigid example of selfless heroism as in the *Birkenhead*, when a line was drawn between the troops and the passengers.

It is the way men should behave at sea. That some have broken under the final strain is not surprising, but

Birkenhead's example must have helped many to maintain control when all else seemed hopeless.

Blessed as we are with hindsight, it is hard to picture a more degrading contrast to the *Birkenhead* than that of the loss of the frigate *Medusa* in 1816.

As we read of the preparations for her last voyage we could be excused for wondering how she reached as far as she did before calamity and unsurpassed horror marked her down in the sea's history book.

Eighteen-sixteen was a difficult year for France. The war was lost, and Napoleon had been defeated earlier at Waterloo. In accordance with the peace treaty France was to be allowed to take back some of her old African possessions, previously captured by the English during the war. One of them was Senegal, on the West Coast, and in order to wipe out some of the humiliation caused by her defeat, France decided to restore all the old systems of colonial governorship without delay, so that trade could be renewed and the memory of the English occupiers of her territory be eliminated.

The proposed reoccupation was plagued with misfortune from the outset. Discipline in the French Army and Navy was at a very low ebb. This was hardly surprising as many of them felt betrayed by their Revolution and were, in many cases, unwilling to continue serving under officers they considered incompetent, or who had brought about their country's downfall. The officers, too, were bitter and confused, a common enough state of affairs in our own lifetime when a country has been made to accept defeat after years of suffering and all-out effort.

Nevertheless, the voyage of the *Medusa* and her consorts seems to have rated higher than any other sea-drama in matters of negligence and gross incompetence.

Apart from the frigate there were three other ships. The corvette *Echo*, brig *Argus*, and a supply and personnel vessel *La Loire*. Little is known of the latter three ships, although it appears that they were only spared a similar fate to the *Medusa* more by luck than skill.

Medusa was the senior ship, and apart from various re-occupation personnel also carried the new governor of Senegal, a man named Schmaltz. They set sail from Rochefort on June 17th, and things started to go wrong almost at once. The *Medusa* by a complete miscalculation of navigation nearly ran aground in the Bay of Biscay, something which was hard to do in open water.

More navigational errors put the ship on the wrong course and she was soon completely out of sight and contact with both *La Loire* and *Argus*.

Five days after leaving harbour a ship's boy fell overboard and there was a long delay before any real attempt to save him was made. Finally the captain ordered a boat to be lowered. It was a six-oared boat, yet only three seamen went into it, with the result the boy was never seen again.

Some of the ship's gear was apparently rotten, and men were injured unnecessarily by falling to the deck, although little seems to have been done to rectify the faults.

The blame for nearly all these errors, indeed to the subsequent disaster, must lie on the *Medusa*'s captain. Captain Le Chaumareys appears to have been not only unfit for the voyage, but totally unsuitable for command of any kind. An indifferent sailor, callous about his men's welfare, he was accompanied on the voyage by his pretty mistress and a vast stock of wine for his personal use.

He seemed oblivious to the potential powder-keg under his control, even though the ship carried, quite apart from seamen and officials, a motley collection of militia-men, clerks, soldiers of fortune and a few prostitutes for good measure. A total of some 400 people crammed into a small frigate with neither the facilities nor the discipline to keep them in any sort of order.

One man who was to play a vital role in the affair was a young adventurer named Richefort, described vaguely in the records as a 'distinguished member of the Philan-thropic Society of Cape Verde'. Had the captain been keeping an eye open for potential troublemakers he might well have marked the young Richefort down as a sea-lawyer, a man to be watched. But he did not, nor it appears did he show much interest in anything but his mistress and his wine.

Richefort on the other hand was evidently a man of some charm, and soon ingratiated himself with the ship's more important passengers, possibly with an eye on his future in Senegal. One of these passengers was a lawyer named Picard, who was taking with him his family of eight women. Richefort also befriended a middle-aged woman who had once been a highly placed 'camp-follower' much admired by some of Napoleon's officers.

The most extraordinary thing was that Richefort was able to use his charm on the captain to such an extent that Le Chaumareys agreed to hand over the navigational affairs of his ship to him. The crew must have been equally amazed by this state of affairs, and discipline deteriorated accordingly. Even when the main hold caught fire through the carelessness of the ship's baker and nearly set light to the cargo, nothing was done. Next day the same baker caused another fire, but apart from dismantling his oven. little action appears to have been taken against him.

So with Richefort in charge of navigation and the captain spending more and more time in his cabin, the *Medusa* continued on her voyage. The first port of call was Teneriffe, and after that the journey was to take them south along the African coast to their final destination.

Off Cape Blanco, however, about halfway through the proposed voyage, was a great reef. It extended more than 100 miles out to sea and had torn the bottoms out of many ships of every type and nationality before it had been accepted as a real and terrible hazard to navigators.

Captain Le Chaumareys had been instructed verbally and in his written orders to take every step to avoid the reef. It was in fact the main danger to coastal shipping, and due to perverse winds and currents it was not only advisable but necessary to give it a very wide berth, even at the expense of losing time on passage.

But Le Chaumareys did not think it necessary to inform his amateur navigator of this fact. Or if he did, then Richefort chose to ignore the warning.

The only ship still in company, the little corvette *Echo*, was more alert, however, and following at a discreet distance astern soon realised that the frigate was standing into danger and showing no sign of changing tack. Accordingly, *Echo* made several signals to her larger consort, all of which went either unseen or ignored. *Medusa* continued indifferently under a full set of canvas, and after further fruitless attempts to make contact the *Echo* went about to make her own way to Senegal.

One of the passengers, an engineer named Correard, who survived the disaster to write the first full account of the events both before and after the wreck, did understand what was happening, and confided his fears with the lawyer Picard. The latter soon made the news known amongst the other passengers and ship's officers, but Richefort was unimpressed.

Even when a junior officer took soundings and personally confronted him with the evidence that the *Medusa* was indeed sailing into the shallows of a great reef, he refused to order a change of course. It is doubtful if anything which he could do would have made much difference at that stage, but he did not even try to do it.

It is easy to criticise the others for allowing an amateur like Richefort to sail the ship to her death without raising a hand to stop him. But it is often true at such moments that subordinates will look to authority without question, no matter how unlikely that authority may appear.

And so on the afternoon of July 3rd, beneath a bright, clear sky, and hardly any sea running, the frigate *Medusa* ran aground on the reef.

Despite the danger, the actual grounding was deceptively gentle, that part of the reef being covered with hard sand. No timbers were smashed, and after the first confusion had settled, the sails were furled to avoid further unnecessary movement. On the face of it they had been extremely lucky.

The obvious procedure was to lighten ship as much as possible. The guns made up a very great weight, and those, plus the heavy barrels of flour in the main hold, should have been quite sufficient to lighten her enough to float off on the next tide. Then she could either sail carefully away from the reef, or if that was too difficult, then the boats could be lowered to tow her well clear before taking advantage of the wind.

At that moment in time, and only then, Captain Le Chaumareys might have saved his ship and retained command. But emerging on deck like a raging bull he refused to allow a single cannon to be dropped overboard. Likewise, the new governor, Schmaltz, said that the flour, his flour, would stay where it was in the hold.

The captain further insisted that the ship would float off anyway on the next tide, and seemed to show little concern as to why she was so near the reef in the first place.

But he was right about one thing, the ship did float off, and for a few more moments it appeared as if his strange luck was going to last.

Then with a savage shudder the *Medusa* struck again, harder this time, and as the hull shivered to one terrible convulsion after another it was obvious she had merely moved to a different and more formidable part of the reef. Then, as before, the shaking passed, and even the captain at last understood that his ship was gripped firmly and finally by the sand, with no hope of riding free.

The moments which followed swiftly on the grounding were immediate and confusing, even harder for us to understand today.

Some of the ship's seamen seemed to go completely berserk, and chased Richefort up and down companionways, cursing his name and threatening to throw him to the sharks for his stupid incompetence. Some sort of order was eventually restored by armed officers, but not before one of the women passengers had been severely beaten and several of the crew had become helpless with drink.

The chaos and mounting anxiety lasted for a further three days, during which time the ship's company and passengers divided into separate groups to try to decide what to do. The weather was still favourable, and three days would appear ample time to prepare a suitable plan to evacuate the *Medusa* and begin some sort of passage towards the shore.

Instead, bickering and then actual violence flared on every hand. Drunkenness was rife after a spirit room was broached, accusations and counter accusations added to the sense of unreality and growing terror. Then, as if impatient at their behaviour, the sea changed its mood and a storm blew up with surprising suddenness. The rudder broke free from its yoke lines and started to pound from side to side like the tail of a great fish, smashing against and eventually stoving in some of the hull timbers below the waterline. Caught by wind and waves, yet unable to ride with the jerking motion, the poor *Medusa* began to break up. But there were still some aboard who were quite unable to grasp the real seriousness of their situation. Instead of preparing to abandon ship or contain the rising water in the holds they rifled stores and rampaged between decks to break open passengers' luggage. More casks of wine were seized, and men staggered helplessly amongst the confusion of falling spars and rigging, completely devoid of understanding and beyond reason.

In the meantime Captain Le Chaumareys had at last decided on a plan of action. It must be recorded as one of the real examples of sheer incompetence and disorder. Instead of regaining overall command he handed over the ship's six lifeboats to the sole control of Governor Schmaltz, a man who had already shown his callous indifference to other men's lives over the dumping of the flour supply. The boats were supposed to carry a total of 250 persons, a fair proportion in those days when it was assumed there would always be enough seamen, and the trained officers to lead them, who could build rafts for the remainder left aboard a wreck.

But Schmaltz had other, more personal values. He

loaded his own boat with a mass of provisions and possessions, and with a minimum of hands aboard thrust away
from the stricken ship. The remainder of the boats were
mostly taken by Schmaltz's friends or whoever could fight
their way into them. It was turmoil and a wild abandon-
ment of every kind of discipline. In the midst of it,
Captain Le Chaumareys and his lovely mistress, plus a
selection of his better wine, left the ship almost unnoticed
in a heavily guarded boat, leaving the bulk of his men to
fend for themselves as best they could.

Seeing the boats riding free from the ship, some barely
filled, many men leapt overboard and tried to clamber
aboard them for safety. Those lucky enough to reach the
nearest ones were immediately driven off by blows or
actual thrusts from bared swords.

Only the lawyer Picard seemed to keep his head. Left
behind in the pandemonium he obtained a musket and
said he would kill those in the boat closest to the ship if
they did not draw near to receive him and his family. He
got his way, but the remaining survivors were not so
fortunate. Apart from those in the boats and others
drowned or killed trying to reach them, there still remained nearly 200 aboard the listing wreck.

There were few senior seamen left to take charge, and
in the resulting panic it was all they could do even to get
some of the hands to work building a raft while there was
still time.

It was a hopeless affair, built of fallen topmasts, planks
and spars, and lashed together with all kinds and thick-
nesses of rope, and measured some sixty feet by twenty.
As the men struggled to get it lowered over the side they
were hampered by crazed figures who charged about the
decks in hopeless disorder, while others persisted in diving

into the sea as if still in hopes that the boats would pick them up.

A total of 147 people crammed themselves on to the raft, leaving behind on the wreck some seventeen drunken passengers and sailors who were too incapable even to fight for a place.

The raft, overloaded to the last inch, started to sink immediately. When it reached its natural buoyancy all the passengers were standing waist-deep in water, clinging to each other in a great human mass.

Le Chaumareys, seeing that his men had been split into more manageable numbers, decided once again to resume command. Shouting his orders from boat to boat he informed all within earshot that he would take the raft in tow and proceed as before to Senegal.

It is difficult to know if the *Medusa*'s captain was as stupid as he appeared or merely cunning. He may have been meaning to show that he was at least trying to save life so that his name could be spared at any future investigation.

Either way, the raft broke adrift from the hasty tow after only a short while, and ignoring the cries and screams from those on board Le Chaumareys and his well-provisioned boats hoisted their sails and made off on their own.

The raft had no proper sails or rigging of any sort, and only a tiny portion of drinking water and a few ship's biscuits. There was, however, a good supply of wine in several casks, and within hours some of the survivors were fighting drunk, and this aboard a raft still submerged under its great weight of human cargo.

An officer had managed to bring a small compass with him, but it was lost overboard in the fighting and scuffling around him. During that first dreadful night twenty persons fell overboard, either killed or too drunk to care what happened. But the raft rose a little higher, and for a few hours it did appear there might still be some hope of regaining calm. By nightfall again, however, the picture changed for the worse. There were a good few soldiers on the raft, and getting together they decided that if they were to die they would at least go in one last, mad celebration. Smashing open a whole cask of wine they proceeded to get insanely drunk, and mutinied against the remaining officers like wild animals.

It is only too easy to picture the pitiful and frightening scene of horror. A handful of sober men fighting against a crazed mob of rioters, all of them reeling and stabbing at each other while submerged knee-deep in the sea.

During the battle the woman camp-follower was hurled overboard but rescued by the engineer who had first seen *Medusa*'s danger at the reef.

By daylight only sixty-seven remained on the raft, some sixty having been killed in the battle. The survivors were then faced with the new horrors of raging thirst and hunger. The biscuits had gone, not that there were enough in the first place for more than a handful of men, and as the sun rose high to add to the torture some started to gnaw at belts and leather lashings, and others drove themselves beyond reason by drinking salt water.

There was worse to come. One corpse from the last crazed fight had remained pinned between the spars of the raft, and after some further hesitation a few of the survivors drew their knives and fell on it like butchers. After the first natural revulsion at what they had done cannibalism became the rule rather than the exception. Ragged, terrified and driven beyond human reason they fought each other, the survivors using the victims to sustain them through the next hours.

By the fourth day only forty-eight remained alive, and then another mutiny exploded, this time the motley of soldiers and passengers drawing together to fight with the officers. Eighteen more died and many were wounded, and once more the poor camp-follower was thrown overboard. How she had survived that long says much for her endurance. She was saved by the officers who somehow managed to overwhelm their attackers.

By the seventh day, however, things had reached an impossible state of degradation and despair. Only twenty-seven were alive, and after a cold appraisal of the situation it was decided that there was only enough wine left to support fifteen persons. A council was formed, and the chosen few examined the sick and wounded amongst those on the raft. The twelve weakest, including the camp-follower, were then thrown to the waiting sharks without further speculation or pity.

The fifteen who remained drifted on, day after day, under a relentless sun and without sign of help. Sometimes they caught flying fish and mixed them with human flesh to make the latter more palatable. Weak, half-mad, they still managed to find some inner strength to vent their anger and despair on one another. During the day they were too dazed by sun and thirst to rest, and at night too terrified to sleep in case one or more became the raft's next human meal.

Yet, somehow, the remainder did survive, and thirteen days after the wreck the raft was sighted by the little brig *Argus* returning from Senegal to find out what had happened to them.

Curiously, there appears to have been little action taken

against the callous Captain Le Chaumareys, nor apparently were any steps made to bring Governor Schmaltz to justice for his behaviour. Schmaltz was later to throw some light upon what had happened to the seventeen luckless souls who had been left aboard the *Medusa* when the raft and boats abandoned her. His reasons, however, were for profit rather than any kind of humanity.

He had left in the *Medusa*'s hold a good deal of money and stores, somehow overlooked by his servants when they had quit the wreck, and he was quite determined to recover them.

He despatched a schooner to find his possessions, if at all possible, and over seven weeks after the actual shipwreck the little vessel anchored close to the reef and the battered hulk of the *Medusa*.

The boarding party, to their horror, found three men still aboard, stark mad, and in the last stages of survival. Only one of them lived to tell his story ashore, and it makes a fitting ending to the *Medusa*'s disaster.

Crazed with drink and numb with fear the men left aboard the wreck had lived like animals. Each one chose a private corner in the hull, which he rarely left unless to hunt for food. The latter was almost non-existent, and they were soon made to eat tallow candles and a few shreds of salt pork. But there was a great deal of wine still aboard the wreck, and whenever these scavengers chanced to meet one another they would fight to the death with knives or clubs, until only the three found by the schooner remained.

In spite of the damage to his mind and body the one survivor managed to gain strength on his passage back to Senegal, and by the time he was taken ashore he was speaking almost lucidly about what had happened.

The authorities in Senegal had been stunned by the

news of the wreck, more so at what had happened afterwards. Urged on by public anger and concern it was decided to help the last survivor to return to France, where added to the horror of the raft it might do the most good in preventing anything like it happening again.

But the very night before he was due to take passage for France he was killed in his bed, and his silent murderer never found. The fact that neither Le Chaumareys nor Schmaltz were ever charged with their deeds rather points to the likelihood that the lone survivor knew too much for his own safety. In all fairness it must be said that there were many others who wished the story to die. It was too dreadful, too gruesome to be prolonged by investigation and discussion, and was best forgotten. Like so many stories of the sea, however, it did not fade, and the name *Medusa* can still raise a chill and a feeling of shame for her and her company.

And what of young Richefort, of the Philanthropic Society of Cape Verde, the man who blithely sailed his temporary command to her doom on the reef? He was never heard of again, and under the circumstances it is hardly surprising.

Heroism and horror, the two widest extremes of survival at sea, yet how narrow the margin of safety between them.

Index